TOOLS FOR THESE TIMES

*Timely Sermons in Uncertain Times*

# Tools for These Times

*Timely Sermons in Uncertain Times*

TOOLS FOR THESE TIMES

# Tools for These Times

## Timely Sermons in Uncertain Times

by

Minister

Onedia N. Gage

TOOLS FOR THESE TIMES

*Timely Sermons in Uncertain Times*

# Other Books By Onedia N. Gage

As We Grow Together Daily Devotional for Expectant Couples

As We Grow Together Prayer Journal for Expectant Couples

The Blue Print: Poetry for the Soul

In Purple Ink: Poetry for the Spirit

Living An Authentic Life

Love Letters to God from a Teenage Girl

The Measure of a Woman: The Details of Her Soul

On This Journey Daily Devotional for Young People

On This Journey Prayer Journal for Young People

One Day More Than We Deserve Daily Devotional for the Growing Christian

One Day More Than We Deserve Prayer Journal for the Growing Christian

Promises, Promises: A Christian Novel

Yielded and Submitted: A Woman's Journey for a Life Dedicated to God

Yielded and Submitted: A Woman's Journey for a Life Dedicated to God Prayers and Journal

*Library of Congress*

## Tools for These Times:

## Timely Sermons in Uncertain Times

All Rights Reserved © 2013

Onedia N. Gage

No part of this of book may be reproduced or transmitted in Any form or by any means, graphic, electronic, or mechanical, Including photocopying, recording, taping, or by any Information storage or retrieval system, without the Permission in writing from the publisher.

Purple Ink, Inc. Press

For Information address:
Purple Ink, Inc
P O Box 41232
Houston, TX 77241
www.purpleink.net
www.onediagage.com

ISBN:

978-1-939119-23-0

Printed in United States

# God's Word

## His Tools for Us

[14] How, then, can they call on the one they have not believed in? And how can they believe in the one of whom they have not heard? And how can they hear without someone preaching to them? [15] And how can they preach unless they are sent? As it is written, "How beautiful are the feet of those who bring good news!"

**Romans 10:14-15**

[6] We have different gifts, according to the grace given to each of us. If your gift is prophesying, then prophesy in accordance with your[a] faith; [7] if it is serving, then serve; if it is teaching, then teach; [8] if it is to encourage, then give encouragement; if it is giving, then give generously; if it is to lead,[b] do it diligently; if it is to show mercy, do it cheerfully.

**Romans 12:6-8**

Therefore, since through God's mercy we have this ministry, we do not lose heart. [2] Rather, we have renounced secret and shameful ways; we do not use deception, nor do we distort the word of God. On the contrary, by setting forth the truth plainly we commend ourselves to everyone's conscience in the sight of God. [3] And even if our gospel is veiled, it is veiled to those who are perishing. [4] The god of this age has blinded the minds of unbelievers, so that they cannot see the light of the gospel that displays the glory of Christ, who is the image of God. [5] For what we preach is not ourselves, but Jesus Christ as Lord, and ourselves as your servants for Jesus' sake.

**2 Corinthians 4:1-5**

TOOLS FOR THESE TIMES

# Dedication

For the ears who hear

For the hearts who adhere

For the souls which are healed

TOOLS FOR THESE TIMES

# Dear Sister and Brother:

Greetings in the name of our Lord and Savior Jesus Christ! I am hoping this work finds you searching for more of Jesus. In the following pages, we seek to grow closer to Christ Jesus. Daily, I seek more of God, Jesus and the Holy Spirit. Many days I am successful. Some days I am not.

As I have prepared each of these sermons with the leadership and guidance of the Holy Spirit, I hope these words and messages bless your life, your message, and your ministry. I consider that you are holding these messages by divine providence. Use this for what God has designed—a walk closer with Him.

Each of these sermons has a distinct message for us. Read and study carefully for each of these messages and how they relate to your current situations and circumstances.

May these words bless you. May they enrich your life. May they lift your spirit. May they address your soul. May they encourage your ministry. May they provide accountability for your commitment to Christ. May they convict you in your worship.

$^{24}$ """The LORD bless you
  and keep you;
$^{25}$ the LORD make his face shine upon you
  and be gracious to you;
$^{26}$ the LORD turn his face toward you
  and give you peace.'" Numbers 6:24-26. NIV84

Amen.

In Christ's Service,

*Onedia N Gage*

Minister Onedia N. Gage

# Dear Father God,

May the words of my heart and the meditations of my heart be pleasing in Your sight. Psalm 19:14.

May You offer me forgiveness of my sins. Please do not allow Your words which you have gifted me with to be hindered by me and any of my "STUFF."

Lord, thank You for the gift of preaching, teaching, and service You have gifted into me. May you remind me to remain meek and humble everyday and particularly when I approach the pulpit to preach and teach and pray.

Thank You for blessing my life with the messages You first gave to minister to my spirit within these pages.

I pray for those who will hold these pages. I pray their strength and healing, their love and spirituality. I pray You draw them closer to You as they study these messages; even more so than me and my closeness to You.

Lord, thank You for our salvation and the gift of Your Son, Jesus Christ!

Lord, thank You for loving me in spite of my "ugly" self! Thank You for urging me to love others, live out loud before others, especially those who despitefully use me, and keep me loving others in spite of my desire not to.

## Tools for These Times

Lord, finally thank You for the gift and power of prayer. Remind us, urge us that we pray daily to You, seeking Your will, love and leadership. Lest I be reminded that I seek and "chase" Your approval daily.

Because You Loved me First, God,

*Onedia*

Your Daughter

Onedia

*Timely Sermons in Uncertain Times*

# Table of Contents

Letter to the Reader

Prayer

Sermons

> Because He Loves Her
> Ephesians 3:14-21
> 21
>
> I'm All In
> Ephesians 3:14-21
> 35
>
> You Have a Heart Condition
> 1 Samuel 16:7
> 45
>
> An Inordinate Strength in Ordinary Times
> Isaiah 40:28-30
> 57
>
> The Storm's Lessons
> Mark 4:35-41
> 71
>
> On a Mission of Service
> John 13:1-17
> 81
>
> When Your Plan to Sin Fails
> 1 Corinthians 10:13
> 93

Your Back Should Hurt
Matthew 11:28-30
105

Your Faith Has Made You Whole
Luke 8:50, 8:48, Matthew 15:28
115

Your Destiny Cannot Be Avoided
Romans 8:28-39
129

Better Than I Know Myself
Psalm 139:1-4
145

God's GPS is Not Broken
Psalm 139:5-6
155

Haters Will Not Stop Hating... So Quit Asking
John 15:18-19
167

FDIC Not Necessary
2 Corinthians 5:5
183

New Year, New You
Acts 9:1-22
195

Resources

Acknowledgements

About the Minister

*Timely Sermons in Uncertain Times*

# Tools for These Times

TOOLS FOR THESE TIMES

# BECAUSE HE LOVES HER

**Ephesians 3:14-21** New International Version (NIV)

**A Prayer for the Ephesians**

[14] For this reason I kneel before the Father, [15] from whom every family[a] in heaven and on earth derives its name. [16] I pray that out of His glorious riches he may strengthen you with power through His Spirit in your inner being, [17] so that Christ may dwell in your hearts through faith. And I pray that you, being rooted and established in love, [18] may have power, together with all the Lord's holy people, to grasp how wide and long and high and deep is the love of Christ, [19] and to know this love that surpasses knowledge—that you may be filled to the measure of all the fullness of God.

[20] Now to Him who is able to do immeasurably more than all we ask or imagine, according to His power that is at work within us, [21] to Him be glory in the church and in Christ Jesus throughout all generations, forever and ever! Amen.

## THE SERMON

Does she know that He loves her? Not because of what He gave her or what He gave him to give her. Does she know that He loves her? Not because of what she looks like or what she does or doesn't do. Does she know that He loves her? His love is available regardless of when she is angry or sad or disappointed or happy or delighted. Does she know that He loves her? When the world turns its back on her very existence, He still loves her but is she aware? Does she know that He loves her in spite of her sins and her shortcomings, her idiosyncrasies and her drama? Does she know that He loves her when you don't?

Does she know that He loves her unconditionally? Does she know that He loves her when you come home late? Does she know that He loves her when you can't talk to her? Does she know that He loves her when she doesn't love herself? Because nobody showed her. And nobody will. Does she know that He is her definition of love? And you are not in your finite manner her definition of anything other than how to love Him and even that lacks the attention that He deserves.

Does she know how to look for His love from Him and only Him? The kind of love that only He can deliver and fulfill and cultivate because He made her and will only love her through her storms and her uncertainty and her difficulties and her pain. Does she know His love and its boundaries and its limits and its uncertainties? Because there are none. He has no boundaries and He has no limits and He has no uncertainties.

Does she know that He loves her and has work for her to do? Does she know that she has a calling on her life to serve Him with everything she has and when she thinks she is unworthy, He will lift her up to serve Him? Because He loves her. Does she know the price of her life? Does she know what it cost Him to love her? Does she know the cost of her sins on that Cross?

## Because He Loves Her

Her behavior says no. Her eyes read I want to know that love. Her body begs to know that love, otherwise it might fall across enemy lines. Her mind suggests that there is such a love but her heart cannot find. Her heart has been misled several times. I know that she doesn't know because I watched her all year at school. I am her teacher.

I teach math in public school to $7^{th}$ graders. By Gage's definition of a $7^{th}$ grader, they are walking evidence that the love that should be boundlessly evident in their lives stopped at some point. They stopped loving. They stopped being loved. Someone gave up because of the attitude they present. Others gave up because the $7^{th}$ grader rejected them. They stopped using the definition of the person that first held them at their birth because they never got the reinforcement of that love. They stopped using the definition of the persons who genuinely love them and want nothing from them because they cannot find them now. They only know love which is attached with not simply strings but attached by the entire rope from which that string is unraveled. I watch them walk around defining themselves by others who want to define them if they could find themselves with a mirror and a flashlight. They have no self-esteem. They think you can buy self-esteem in a bottle or on a hanger.

As a teacher, I have the summer off but I have some homework to do. I have to share with a young girl, who will one day be in the $7^{th}$ grade or is already past the $7^{th}$ grade, the authentic definition of love. How am I to do this for someone who has otherwise advertised themselves as unlovable or unloving or the unwelcoming recipient of such love? Well as a disciple of Christ, He says to us in John 8:34-35: "A new command I give you: Love one another. As I have loved you, so you must love one another. By this [love] all men will know that you are my disciples, if you love one another." Then as Jesus reappears to the disciples after the resurrection, He says in Matthew 28:19-20: "Therefore go and make disciples of all nations, baptizing them in the name of the Father and of the Son and of the Holy Spirit, and teaching them to obey everything I have commanded you." This would include love. Because of the obstacles that may present themselves, I need some help. Can you help me with my homework? I pulled some resources together today for our assignment. I brought the dictionary, the Bible and some paper.

Webster's dictionary defines love as a strong affection and indicates that love in this definition is a noun. The dictionary notes that love is also expressed as the "fatherly concern of God for humankind." Gage defines love in only the verb tense as an action; an action indicating the depth, width, height, and length of that love. "What can you do to show me that you love me? If you love me, prove it." says Gage. Children generally speaking define love as T I M E. "How much is your time worth? Can I have some?"

Jesus defines love for us through His actions and His time. Jesus teaches us how to love. He shares His definition of the reciprocal love He wants with us. The Lord has spent time on making sure that He has given us every possible reason to know that He loves us, but everyone still doesn't know. As His disciple, that is our job.

One of the first scriptures that children learn is John 3:16. This is the first definition of love we will share. I think she can remember "For God so loved the world that He gave His One and Only Son that whosoever believes in Him shall not perish but have eternal life." She has to understand that God gave Mary a Son to birth for Him. Mary mothered Him until He was old enough to preach. When He was old enough, she found Him in the synagogue. He then traveled with 12 hand selected disciples. One betrayed Him. He died for our sins so that we would not die for our own sins. That should help her understand love. She needs to know another way that He demonstrates His love for us.

He washed the disciples' feet. This would be an extension of His love. He was explaining that when He washed their feet that they were clean. This foot washing was a service to them. They needed to know this so that they could pass this along to other believers and even none believers so that the love of Christ would be experienced. This sacrificial love displayed that Jesus knew each of us and realized that we need some special attention. I think that she can remember John 13:14: "Now that I, your Lord and Teacher, have washed your feet, you also wash one another's feet." Sometimes this is not an actual washing but also a proverbial washing so that the other person experiences the love of Christ through your sacrificial service to them. But if that is not enough, then I will talk about Jesus leaving the Holy Spirit.

Jesus left us the Holy Spirit. I think she can remember John 14:26: "But the Counselor, the Holy Spirit, whom the Father will send in my name, will teach you all things and remind you of everything I have said to you." Jesus left us the Holy Spirit to dwell within and indwell with us. The Holy Spirit fills us and leaves no empty spaces. I think we could bring a vase filled with rocks, explaining that these are her insides. I will then explain that the sand I am pouring in the vase is the Holy Spirit who is filling all of the spaces she previously felt and saw. Then she will understand the space the Holy Spirit will occupy. She will need to know that leaving the Holy Spirit is an act of love by Jesus. This is the truest form of love. When she cannot remember the Holy Spirit, then she will need to know about the reciprocity of love.

Jesus states in John 14:13: "If you love Me, you will obey what I command." This is the definition of loves' reciprocity. When He loves us, He does sacrificial acts for us. He washed our feet, He left us the Holy Spirit, He died for our sins and He heals the sick, among other things. He has asked that if we love Him, then we should obey His commands. Our obedience is what He needs from us. He knows sometimes that we have battles so that we can obey, but He is faithful and just and will come to our rescue at any time. I think she can remember John 14:13. Once she understands that reciprocity, she needs to understand her purpose in life.

God created us in His image for several reasons. One of which is to praise Him. The scripture I think she can remember is Psalm 8:2: "From the lips of children and infants you have ordained praise." She will learn to praise as He draws her closer through His love and time He spends with her. She will grow to praise Him in all occasions and in all seasons. She will praise Him to share her love with Him. Once she praises Him for who He is and His unconditional love which has changed her life, she will understand her self-esteem is only under His review.

When she realizes that she is defined by Him because she was made in His image, His likeness, I think it would be impossible to for her not to memorize Psalm 139:14: "I praise You because I am fearfully and wonderfully made; your works are wonderful and I know that full well." She will understand that her self-esteem, her self-image is defined by God, rather than anybody else. She will learn to cast away the definition that others would like for her to espouse. Instead, she will consider her features in the mirror and be reminded that God has a purpose for those features and all that she is inside and out. His breath that He breathed into her will not return void. She will understand that she is not arrogant but filled with the love of Jesus, the indwelling of the Holy Spirit and created by God. Next, she will need to know about the work she will do.

God has plans for her and she has a job. God gave each of us a job at creation. She needs to know that she is worthy and expected to do God's will and His work. The scripture she should memorize is Ephesians 2:10: "For we are God's workmanship, created in Christ Jesus to do good works, which God prepared in advance for us to do." This reminds her that she is accountable to others for the work God has for her to do. She needs to remember that God planned her existence with the beginning of creation. She will be reminded that she was not an afterthought, nor a mistake. She will acknowledge that Christ is never far away. Lastly, she needs a lesson in faith.

"Now faith is the substance of things hoped for, the evidence of things not seen." Hebrews 11:1. It may take her awhile to completely comprehend the faith definition but the important point is that she remembers Hebrews 11:6 which reads: "But without faith it is impossible to please God, because anyone who comes to him must believe that he exists and that he rewards those who earnestly seek him." She needs to believe He is God. Then earnestly seek Him in all that she is and does.

She needed all of those lessons so she could handle the text. The text teaches several lessons. Ephesians is one of my favorite books of the Bible. The teachings are so practical and concise. The lessons Paul presents to the Ephesians are timeless.

The first lesson for her is that Christ dwells in her heart. Verses 16-17a teaches her that God's glorious riches provide the Holy Spirit with power so that Christ may dwell in her heart through faith. The Spirit dwells within us to provide guidance, to teach us what Christ would have us to do, to offer us comfort, and to offer us wise counsel. All of this is impossible without faith. Nothing can happen if she doesn't believe. Consider you at her age. What was your faith like at her age? Did you know what faith was? Did you know how to exercise your faith? Did you know how to recognize when your faith has manifested itself into existence? Who is showing her their faith? And who is explaining to her what their faith means?

Who is telling her that they have faith in her? Who is encouraging her to keep believing in herself? Who is sharing with her that the Lord believes in her because He made her and is completely certain of what she is capable of and is waiting on her to do exactly that? If we are not answering "me" to those questions then we are shirking our responsibilities. It is our job to share with her God's power that fuels her faith.

The second lesson for her is that she was already rooted and established in love. When she relinquished her very first definition of love, we made a mistake. Since that error we have to take great steps to re-establish the default settings. Now Paul is praying that she may have power and that she would join with other believers to grasp, clutch, to lay hold of with the mind, handle, embrace, comprehend, to seize eagerly, the measure of the love of Christ. Verse 18 reads " . . . to grasp how wide and long and high and deep is the love of Christ," Paul is praying for her to have the power to understand the measure of the love of Christ. Paul defines the love of Christ to have depth and height and width and length. In mathematical terms, this would be a calculation of surface area and volume, which combined is capacity. This is a combination of formulas that would easily calculate His love if there were some actual measurements that we could place on that diagram. And who can calculate infinity anyway?

However, we are dealing with the love of Christ. The love that puts us to sleep us at night and that lets us sleep through our worry, pain and guilt. The love when Christ wraps His arms around us when we cannot breathe because we are depressed or anxious or both. The love of Christ which shelters us from life's inevitable storms. The love which prevents us from failing and falling and faltering and floundering. The love that congratulates us when we have done what He commanded us to do. The love of Christ that was there all the time.

The third lesson is the knowledge that His love surpasses her knowledge. We cannot actually comprehend all of His love but if we just experience the residual of His love it is still more than enough to make us whole and complete. Verse 19 reads, "and to know this love that surpasses knowledge—that you may be filled to the measure of all the fullness of God." One theologian said that in order to fill us with His love, a thimble would suffice in comparison. His love is more than we deserve yet we have it anyway. She has to understand, by looking at me, that God loves her even when she sins and feels unworthy and when you have put her down and rejected her. He wants me to share with her His love for her. And you are supposed to do the same. So anyone ready to do so?

The fourth lesson is committing all of it back to the Creator. Verse 20 Paul offers praise and glory with these words, "Now unto Him who is able to do exceeding abundantly above all that we ask or think, according to His power that is at work in us." Paul is clear and wants the church of Ephesus to be completely clear that God can do all that but there also has to be God's power at work within us—not by our own power or might or will. By the way, not only can we not out love God, we cannot out think God either. She is supposed to be taught that love from God will continue to exist and no one can keep that love from her. Not even her. She also needs to be reminded that there is God's power at work within her. She needs to be shown how to access and use God's power that is in her. She will know from this what God thinks of her. She needs to know that God thinks of her with love and nothing else. She needs to realize that the great things He has for her to do will be powered by Him through her. She is not in charge of and has no power over those events, happening or not happening. This is the point that always arrests my attention: God's power is the **only** power and my efforts of stimulus or sabotage will not interfere with His power.

Lastly, verse 21 suggests that the generations to follow will give Him glory forever and ever. In order for this to happen, we have to teach her that He loves her first. He loves her completely. He loves her unconditionally: Because He desires to love her. If she doesn't understand the legacy of love, then the following generations will be lost and unloved. They will not know how to seek the love of God because they won't know God. We have to teach her to love God so that she will teach others to love Him.

When we are teaching math, one of the things that comes with higher order math is that we prove the facts. We prove the postulate or the theorem or the theory or the formula. Once we have shown them the mathematical proof then the students understand the concept better. We attach the playground to the classroom. If we want her to understand the love of Christ, we have to teach it to her and show her and re-teach her and retell her and show her until she is the model for the love of Christ.

When she is the model, then and only then will we have a legacy.

Jesus' love offers her the opportunity to thrive and thirst for the approval of another no more.

With His love then she can ask what the rest of us have already tested:

> How high will Your love stretch
>
> How long will Your love last
>
> How wide will Your love span
>
> How deep will Your love extend

When she asks, she knows that He will answer her in a way that no one can or will. When she asks, she asks with the understanding that He has already defined love for her.

When she can use Jesus' definition of love, my homework will earn an A. By the way, thanks for your help. When she walks with Him and they have a relationship that is uninterrupted and unadulterated by others, I know that I did a great job as a Christian. I have authentically shared His love which I didn't always access or understand. I'll know that she knows love because her voice will be charismatic and her words will be cultivated. She will know that He wants her to rely on Him for all her needs. She will know to access the Holy Spirit in her time of trouble and pain, grief and sorrow. She will know that the Holy Spirit is in her and with her at all times. She will know because she accepted Him into her life as her personal Savior and Lord.

She knows that He is present and comforts her because she prays and He answers. She will know His love of her. She will know that His love is pure and unconditional because she knows His words. Voice. She will know that the words were meant for her because she knows she is made in His image, not that of someone else's. She will know not to compare herself to others. She will know that He loves her because He answers her when she calls His name. She will know that He loves her because He spends time with her. He will know that she loves Him because she will obey Him. When she doesn't obey, she will ask Him to forgive and He will forgive. And restore. And retain. And in spite of it all, He will still love her.

Amen.

# I'M ALL IN

**Ephesians 3:14-21** New International Version (NIV)

**A Prayer for the Ephesians**

[14] For this reason I kneel before the Father, [15] from whom every family in heaven and on earth derives its name. [16] I pray that out of his glorious riches he may strengthen you with power through his Spirit in your inner being, [17] so that Christ may dwell in your hearts through faith. And I pray that you, being rooted and established in love, [18] may have power, together with all the Lord's holy people, to grasp how wide and long and high and deep is the love of Christ, [19] and to know this love that surpasses knowledge—that you may be filled to the measure of all the fullness of God.

[20] Now to him who is able to do immeasurably more than all we ask or imagine, according to his power that is at work within us, [21] to him be glory in the church and in Christ Jesus throughout all generations, for ever and ever! Amen.

## THE SERMON

I love board games but I don't know how to play poker. It's interesting that the state where gambling is illegal has a most popular poker game named for it, Texas Hold 'Em. I have no idea what separates this game from other poker games and consequently the rules. I learned of poker watching the Celebrity Poker show a few years ago. I learned one of my favorite phrases and my motto: "I am all in." Those words in poker indicate that the player has put all of her money in for the support of her cards. She believes and has complete confidence in her cards that they will beat all else on the table. She is telling the other players that I have what you desire: the best confidence at the table. The "I am all in" happens in two steps: one is the act of pushing the money to the middle of the table, but the most significant part is the announcement which accompanies that action. This is the immediate accountability. In this example it is about cards, but what do you give all that you are and all of what you have and all of what you know? What about love? Do you give all in your love for others? What gets your "all in" attitude? Shopping and sports do not count. What do you have confidence to give all that you are and all that you have to?

There are three things that Paul makes very clear to us here in the verses: 1) God loves us; 2) There is power within us to love and do what He assigned us to do; 3) Our inner being—Our Soul—is important to Him. What is often overlooked in these scriptures is what we are responsible for: our inner being—Our Soul—has to be strong so that Christ may dwell within us. This implies that if we are weak, Christ cannot dwell within us. How do we know if Our Soul is strong? Because sometimes we are without faith, how can Christ live in "our inner being" while we are doubting and without faith? How much is the measure of love on which we survive: wide and long and high and deep is the love of Christ? Why do we choose to live on so much less than what God offers?

It sounds like God is All In. Well all evidence supports that He is. He has done some things which supports that He is All In. That He will give all that He has for us. But are we all in for Him? Most evidence would say no, yet He still loves us. That sounds like only something God can do. We abandon those regularly who do not show or share or support us in the manner we desire or deserve. The God we serve does this over and over again. The question today is how can I give my all to God. Who do I give His love to? What does God want me to do with what and who He has given me? What does my all consist of?

**POWER IS A GIFT**

**THERE IS POWER PLACED IN MY INNER BEING SO THAT I MAY HAVE FAITH.**

Power is an interesting word which is so often missed and misplaced. The word power here refers to the unseen force and hand of God which is the driving force to accomplishments. The scripture states that the power is there to strengthen. Power is only necessary when work is going to be done. The power that is at work within us. What is the power working on within us? What will the power be used for outside of us? Well the power that is at work within us is so that we can understand God, what He has called us to do and how He would like that work to be accomplished. The power we display outside is to share His power with others to help them discover what God wants for them. The power He gives us is the same but the uses will be different.

In order for that inner being to be effective to receive and distribute this education, the inner being has to be in working order. The inner being, or Soul, if you will, has to be healthy. How do I know if my soul is healthy? The answer is what comes out of your mouth and your mind and your heart. The computer adage "garbage in, garbage out" is true here as well. If you only put garbage in, you will get garbage out. What do you put on your mind, what do you listen to, what do you read, and what do you repeat to yourself about yourself. Those questions open the doors to some very powerful information. This will direct you to the changes God expects. The management of this information is important so that your soul can prosper. For most of us, we hear a lot of negativity. What do you do to counteract that negativity? Nothing? You do nothing when you listen to music which does not talk about you in a positive manner or listen to someone who asks you what part of the fault is yours. There is nothing wrong with accountability but there is something wrong with the manner in which it is proposed. The idea here is that you change the station on your radio or your mp3 player or your friends and sometimes your family to something which states emphatically that you are a child of God and that you are worthy of love and forgiveness. Rather than you are the object of the some crazy whim of someone else. For this reason for many years I didn't listen to secular music. I was at a low point in my life and I didn't need the outside noise to add to the attitude I had developed. The soul is important. We have to protect it from the harm which could come if we leave it unprotected. The devil wants your soul to make his argument to God stick.

Faith is required. We know this. Hebrews 11:6 states that without faith it is impossible to please God. We cannot do what we want if we do not have faith in Him. Power and strength causes that faith to grow and manifest itself according to what He needs from us. Paul designates that the strength and power in the inner being so that there is no confusion. This is not for body mass or brute force. This is the internal mechanism which is so much more important than physical characteristics.

### TO GRASP AND TO KNOW REQUIRES A SPECIAL POWER

Paul is always in prayer for us. This occasion is no different. The prayer Paul prays goes on to share that he wants us to understand God's love. Wow! That is quite the undertaking. How do you understand the length of God's love? How far will God's love take you? How far in front of you will God's love go for your well being and provision? How far will God's love go for your nurture and growth? The answer is still wow. Paul does not expect us to answer that yet Paul expects you to understand that there is love and then there is God's love, which is larger than you will ever understand but you need to know that it exists.

The width of His love covers my sins and my issues, my hurts and pains, my healing and correction, my wisdom and my courage, my heart and my mind, and my spirit and its growth. The width of His love is so wide that I cannot reach either edge in this lifetime. I just have to rest in this fact for the rest of my life. The love He has for me is immeasurable, infinite even. Paul wants us to understand that it exists and that we need to know that it exists.

Again there is love and then there is God's love. The comparison is not close at all and this is not going to change. Now, what does He want us to do with this love He has for us? I am glad you asked. He wants us to say thank you for the love. We need His love to serve others and He fully expects us to do so. We have full use of His love to survive the hate and disdain of others. As I have mentioned before, He loves us when do not love ourselves and definitely when we cannot love others. The love that God gives defines the mark of excellence and will not be reversed. He loves us into, during and out of our storms. The love is always there through whatever we are seeking, surviving and sustaining. The love of God is not something you can explain to someone in one sentence or one example. The love of God is designed to create in us a pure heart so that we can best serve Him. The love of God is purposed to show a fraction of Him to others so that they may learn to love God as well.

To grasp and to know requires a special power. Just take a moment to reflect on the sin you committed last year this time. Do you remember? Not really? Did you ask for forgiveness? He forgave you and He forgot too! Do you remember what your sibling did to wrong you? Recently? Last year? 10 years ago? Did they ask for forgiveness? Did you forgive them? Yet you remember what they did and will help them recall it too any time you decide. There is love and then there is God's love. Do you remember the hate you have had in your heart for some people? God massaged your soul and spirit, then He gave you "stuff" to do and kept your mind off of that hate. Now it is easier to co-exist. There is love and then there is God's love.

His love is our example and while we may never love with His capacity, He gives us the capacity to love and that love will survive storms and hardships and will perpetuate sunshine and happiness, peace and joy. His love requires us to be all in.

## The Fullness of His Power Requires Our Cooperation

### According to His Power That is at Work Within Us

Did the lights go out? Did you pay the bill? Did you unplug the power cord? Does the cord have a shortage? This is NOT working! Is this what happens when you flip a switch in your house and nothing happens? I was in my truck recently and my ipod would not play. I was devastated! I tried to troubleshoot the device. After a few tests, I concluded that the cord which connects the device and the truck was the problem. There was a short in the cord. The cord needed to be replaced in order for the power to be restored. The power that is at work within us needs maintenance for us to remain effective. The power comes from God so we need to stay focused on Him. He is the source so we need to stay closely connected to the source.

What do you do to stay connected in relationship with others? You talk on the phone, you text, you email, you send pictures. Some of you are still mailing letters through the postal service! The options are endless really. The point is that you are making a huge effort to spend time with another person which you like and care about and you are doing just that. What do you do for God? Does He get the leftover time? Does He get the absentee presence at church? Does He come after the excuses which keep you from Bible study and those excuses rank up there with 8-track tapes. For those of you who do not know what an 8-track tape is then my point is well illustrated. That reason for not attending Bible study is so outdated and irrelevant that is should be retired and changes should be made to figure out how to make it to Bible study. Just because He loves you!

Love is an intimate relationship requiring time and energy, power and strength. When we are loving God, our time is required to grow closer. As a person who loves time and attention, I can recall relationships which dissipated because we stopped making an effort to communicate and relate to the other person. Okay let me get closer. We have caller identification now so that we can see who is calling and thus can make a decision about whether we want to take that person's call. Sometimes we answer and sometimes we don't. But there are times we answer and we have an emptiness on the other end because we are wondering why is this person calling. They know we don't have a great relationship. God COULD say the same. We call Him when we need Him but we don't stop to hear from Him in between those times.

Love offers a certain amount of accountability. That is the measure of the power that is at work within us. When you are sure of His love, you don't leave Him for days at a time. He knows my heart we say. But do you know your own heart? Do you know the good and bad you are capable of—certainly not! You are only able to refer to what your history states. God knows the rest of your story. Be present!

## CONCLUSION

I am working to be all in on a daily basis. Can you join me? Jesus was all in. He carried that cross when He could have quit. He let them whip Him when He could have cast them dead. He died on that cross when He could have said no. He rose on Sunday with answers we didn't have. I am working to be all in. This is no game. He could have quit. He could have quit on the hill with the cross or on the cross or at the piercings or anytime but He kept His word. Will you be all in for God? Join me to love Christ with all that you are and all that you are not.

    He just wants all of us.

Amen.

# YOU HAVE A HEART CONDITION

**1 Samuel 16:7** New International Version (NIV)

⁷ But the LORD said to Samuel, "Do not consider his appearance or his height, for I have rejected him. The LORD does not look at the things people look at. People look at the outward appearance, but the LORD looks at the heart."

## THE SERMON

The anatomical structure that we call the heart does certain things. The heart pumps the blood throughout the body—all parts. The body cannot operate without a heart—the original, a transplant, or a synthetic one. There are significant uses for the heart and its details. There are surgeons all over the world who are credited as heart surgeons who try to "fix" hearts all day, each day. Some of those surgeries are successful and some are not. Life confirmed results sometimes. Death comes sometimes.

There were 416,000 coronary bypass surgeries in 2009. In 2010, there were 2,300 heart transplants. These doctors have studied for 12 to 16 years to be able to use that label of heart surgeon. Many heart conditions are found as a result of an "event." By event, I mean heart attack, stroke, light headedness, dizziness and high blood pressure or even low blood pressure. An event so monumental that you are parked in the hospital for several days and what is on the phone is no longer as important as it once was.

These surgeries last for hours—long hours where the surgeon could be hungry, tired, sick, emotionally broken or in anyway otherwise distracted. The surgeon is a human being. The surgeon is not God but hopes that his efforts would be God-like character and produce God-like results, even if she does not believe.

## YOU HAVE A HEART CONDITION!

The heart you currently have is in the condition based on the events it had been subjected to: poor eating habits, no exercise, high stress. Am I at your situation yet? These are blamed as stimuli for this heart condition you have developed. The surgeon gets you via recommendation from a general practitioner. The surgeon never sees you first.

The surgeon then can determine what can be done, what the options are, and what will happen on the table. After a successful surgery, then the recovery terms are outlined.

Then there is God.

God created that heart that needs surgery. He didn't create it to need surgery.

Then there is your heart. Your emotions, thoughts, feelings, fears, motives, goals, aspirations, love, hopes, and other miscellaneous feelings. The heart that espouses love and harbors resentment from time to time. The heart that falters when love is in the room. The heart that is broken when loss occurs. The heart that loves God. The heart is a fragile object but not a tangible one. Unlike the organ, which visibly displays damage, the heart does not. The emotional heart covers hurt and disguises pain and harbors unforgiveness. The emotional heart does not show the scars of the past as easily as the stitches from the organ's surgery.

So this emotional heart which has sustained brokenness, pain, hurt, as well as love, forgiveness, and peace, is in need of a Surgeon, a Healer. God is the only one who can do that in our lives.

Our hearts dictate when we are mean or that we are hurt or that we need love and forgiveness.

God recognizes the condition of the heart we have—each of us. We have a heart condition. Hurt, pain, malice, fear, unforgiveness, unforgiven, mean, rude, and broken. The events we have experienced and persons we have encountered affect the degree to which we are damaged.

The heart God created within us loves fully and unconditionally, hopeful and faithful, grateful and gracious, powerful and positive. This heart is a tender place. It is a warm place where people want to experience. This heart is open to new ideas, pure dreams, clear view of the world, and a vision full of hope and promise. That's all available until something happens. That usually happens only at birth. Pain, hurt, disappointment started at birth. There are a few days which do not include hurt, pain, or disappointment. Those few days of life with this pure heart are to be cherished and respected.

The days later in life until the last day of life, God seeks to be our Doctor, our Healer, our Redeemer, and our Authentic Definition of Love, Protection and Forgiveness. God created it to last in its purest form for all of our lives but it did not. The break up in the eleventh grade, the divorce of your parents at six years old, the death of your great-grandmother at the age of twelve, the disappearance of your father, the betrayal of your mother and other family members, the financial trouble, the low self-esteem, the man which broke your heart, the heart you broke, all have driven your heart to need repair; completely overhauled, only God-can-fix-styled-repairs.

You have a heart condition. It is no longer performing with the factory settings. It has evidence of make-shift repairs: tape, glue, string, Velcro, and we tried to dress it up with glitter. The damage coupled with the makeshift repairs determined your motives.

Motive is defined as why I do what I do and what do I gain from the activities in which I engage. If your hurt drives you to hurt others then your motives are not good. If you are motivated by power then you may mistreat others to gain that power.

God considers our heart and its condition. This condition determines how we will behave on our assignment. God fixes our hearts daily—no surgery required.

In the scripture verse, God has sent Samuel to find Him a new king. In this search, God reminds Samuel that the outward appearance is not important. The text teaches us several things starting with outward appearance does not count.

## OUTWARD APPEARANCE DOES NOT COUNT

God created that outward appearance and He is the least impressed with His own work. What we wear and how we match it—our swagger—doesn't impress God. Others are impressed and even motivated by "our swagger." People watch us to see what we wear and how it makes us look. That very appearance has also been the source of many sins—yours and theirs. Yes, I am saying that outward appearance can cause you and others to sin.

Because the outward appearance is so distracting, God ignores it. God rejects it—His own work.

Our outward appearance changes. We gain and lose weight. We get pregnant and it changes shape and sometimes it never returns. Outward appearances are fleeting at best.

God does not care about your physical appearance or the physical attributes. I know that may be hard to understand when He created us but the time He spent on the outside does not compare to the inner being He so wants to be pointed toward Him.

**YOU AND GOD ARE NOT ATTRACTED TO THE SAME THINGS.**

Commonalities do not attract God.

God's thoughts are not our thoughts, God's ways are not our ways is the second point that the text shares with us.

The popular scripture is Isaiah 55:8. It clearly communicates that we are not as great as we think we are. God has a view that we do not have. We have a finite and limited vision of our lives and our days. God knows ALL. Likewise, we need to consider what God wants from us and for us. Consider what we consider important. Challenge yourself about what that is considering what God considers as important.

We do consider good looks to be important. There are many of you who think that we must match and coordinate when we leave home. We have to have on the newest and latest clothes and purses. We consider looks very important. Cosmetics is a multi-billion dollar industry! Botox, cosmetic surgery and weaved hair are very lucrative businesses as well. All for the purposes of changing how we look, feel about how we look, and feel about how we feel about ourselves, so that others will like us better, or so we think and hope.

All that we can judge others by or we can be judged by is our outward appearance. We are not interested in how a person thinks or how they feel or what they need because we don't even know that about ourselves. Besides if we took the time to get to know someone else then we may also have to be transparent. The 11$^{th}$ commandment says avoid transparency at all costs.

Besides all that our outward appearance is the best thing about us anyway. It's the part of us we control. The insides are not a great looking specimen anyway. We use the outward appearance to cover the insides and our brokenness and pain. The outward appearance gives us something to focus on.

Having said all that and knowing what we know, we have a heart condition and we need to change our focus.

Samuel had been walking with God a long time and yet he needed to be reminded that the exterior was his least concern. God reminded Samuel that the exterior was not a measure for how a king would rule God's kingdom. The exterior is the window dressing, like gift wrap or packaging but the gift inside is something you don't want.

God rejects the outward appearance because He loves us inclusive of our faulty insides. God is the only Person that tolerates the vast variation between your Prada, Louis Vitton,

## Tools for These Times

Dooney and Bourke, Franco Sarto, Nordstrom, BMW, Chicos, Jones, well-traveled, well-educated, and decorated outward being and your damaged, muddy, murky, broken, faithlessness, foolishness, misguided, and misdirected insides. God is the only person that is still willing to talk to you even though He knows ALL about you. God is privy (privileged) to know the background of your attitude.

God does know what plagues the depths of your heart. God knows the pain threshold you can bear. God's focus is moving me past my "stuff" to the place where He has planned for me.

God is attracted to your heart so that He can do the impossible with your life.

God ignores my outward appearance.

God has high concerns.

God is looking at my heart.

The condition of my heart is important.

My heart has a condition because it is not whole. It is bruised, broken, bent and in need of healing. There have been times when I feel like my heart was outside of my body and that others can see it for the pain is so great. Likewise, I feel that it is pinned to my shirt so that it is available for attack.

## You Have a Heart Condition

There is a cliché which says that "you are wearing your feelings on your sleeve." This means that you are being openly sensitive about that issue. The problem is that we should be able to be tender in all appropriate situations. The problem is that we are NOT sensitive enough in most scenarios.

God knows that you have been hurt. He knows who has hurt you. He knows the response you gave, and the one you wanted to give. In short God knows the condition of your heart and He knows how it became that way. God does not take your heart for granted. God does not desire you to hurt. He hopes that your hurt will create in you a desire to help others. But that is not what happens. After we are hurt, we stop treating others well and as Jesus would. After we are hurt, we stop loving others. After we are hurt, we stop sharing, communicating, and talking to others. After we are hurt, we consider walking away from God and the Church. After we are hurt, we don't immediately consider forgiveness. After we are hurt, we hurt others. After we are hurt, we forget that God can heal that hurt, that ache, that pain, that brokenness.

God wants to lift the light of your countenance and give you His peace (Numbers 6:26). God can heal and heals your broken, beaten, bruised, and battered heart.

God needs no motive to heal us. God heals us to love Him. Our broken, beaten, battered, and bruised prevents us from properly loving Him. No one is to blame for why we cannot love

God. We simply have been to hurt too much to love God. We are hurt because we have let the wrong people into the protected and secure areas of our lives.

We want to make our way back to God but lack the ability to confess the interruptions and the interferences between us. By committing, we would be forgiven by Him and ourselves. Once we have been excused from our own shame, we could be worthy to approach God to receive His love—unconditional, promised, and necessary.

Bottom line is that God is the only healer of the heart condition. God wants us healed and better. When we are healed back to the factory settings, we are able to love Him, function as a whole being and share Him with others.

Imagine your heart available to love and be loved. When that condition exists, then you are able to be compassionate to God's people, serve God through His people, hear from God and trust Him, share God with others because He is the living water which never runs dry and seek Him earnestly in every situation. Sharing a FULL and complete love through God's healing is a remarkable experience. It allows you to love without prejudice and without fear; without jealousy and without judgment; without liability and without caution.

When He fixes your heart condition, you will be free. Free to submit to His calling on your life without reservation. That's a life worth looking forward to.

## CONCLUSION

When you consider that the physical limitations imposed by a heart condition, you realize that the inappropriate or improper handling could lead to an early death.

Likewise, the continued poor condition of your emotional heart would lead to the walking dead. A physically alive person but an emotionally dead being.

God looks at your heart. Your heart determines your actions and your altitude and functionality in the world. God cares about your heart because this heart is assigned to love. Love the people which He has assigned each of us.

Imagine the fullest capacity of the purest format of your heart. Imagine how much you could achieve, accomplish, overcome, upheave, enhance, elevate, execute, and illuminate with a pure heart and a reconditioned heart.

With your heart's condition being so important to you, it warrants your attention for the Doctor for healing and overall improvement of the condition so that God can select us based on that reconditioned heart.

Amen.

## Tools for These Times

# An Inordinate Strength In Ordinary Times

**Isaiah 40:29-31** New International Version (NIV)

²⁹ He gives strength to the weary
and increases the power of the weak.
³⁰ Even youths grow tired and weary,
and young men stumble and fall;
³¹ but those who hope in the LORD
will renew their strength.
They will soar on wings like eagles;
they will run and not grow weary,
they will walk and not be faint.

## The Sermon

Dictionary.com defines strength as the quality or state of being strong, mental power, and moral power, firmness, or courage. This definition illuminates what we already know: it is the opposite of weak, weary, powerless, down trodden and soft. There are two things which put us on the weak, powerless side of life: a strained relationship with Christ and the reason for which it is strained. Sin separates us from Christ and misunderstanding His love separates us as well. Love produces prayer and prayer provides strength and strength brings power. God wants us to be strong in Him.

Strength for these times is required. The weak will not survive in these times. The stock market is plunging. The heat is unbearable. I am from Texas. The bills are due. The family is unraveling. The government is faltering and not because of lack of leadership. The educational system is failing us and our children. The television is telling us lies we want to believe. The children are questioning who we are and what we are made of, disrespectfully so I might add. We are playing with God. We are challenging Him about trivial issues and we are serious when we do so, blatantly or inadvertently. Where does that strength come from? Where does that "help" come from? It comes from the Lord. Why does He want us to be strong and why is He the only source of that strength?

We have several questions to answer so let's get started.

**WHAT YOU NEED IS ALREADY PRESENT. STOP ASKING FOR WHAT YOU ALREADY HAVE.**

The Bible repeatedly shares with us that what we need we already have. We have or have access to everything we pray for or need. How is that possible? Well I am glad you asked.

We have power. He GIVES it to us! We did not have to ask or earn it. We just HAVE it. We just need to access it. We need to access the provided power. He gives boldness with diplomacy through the Holy Spirit. We just have to access it. Part of this includes no excuses. No second guessing. "I don't have the power. I can't do that." Why do I feel that I don't have power or that I can't do that? Why do I lack that confidence to what God has already empowered me to do?

We have peace. His peace is a gift to us and transcends all of our understandings. It means His peace is bigger than we can imagine. Or self-create. The peace we are expecting is bigger than we understand as well as we often reject the peace He offers us.

We have wisdom. "If anyone lacks wisdom, let him ask and it will be granted." Do we ask? Do we recognize it when it arrives? Do we know what to do with that wisdom?

We have faith. He provides a measure of faith which we have to manage and participate in its increase. We have the faith we need to move mountains but simply deny ourselves access to it.

We have strength. Again this is a gift. An unconditional gift. But we say no thanks. We say no thanks each time we leave the courage of our convictions at home. We say that God is insufficient when we act weak but really possess the gift of His strength. His strength is evident and others see it but we don't use it. That evidence is why we are tested by others. The question they are trying to answer is how strong has He made her and will she allow me to challenge the strength He so willingly provides. My question is how can we consciously doubt and reject but ask again and again?!

We have love. He provided it and a great definition of how love is gained and maintained. We misunderstand it, misjudge it, misappropriate it and mis-appreciate it. Then we misplace and disregard it by giving it to the wrong person, sometimes we are that wrong person, and then we are left wondering why this is not going well. God has actively defined love and we continually give it away inappropriately.

Everything we need is already inside of us so quit misusing and quit asking and start accessing the power, peace, wisdom, faith, strength, and love God has already graciously gifted us with. He promised that He would renew us based on the hope we place on Him so that is an indication that we already have THEM! We allow others to tell us that we don't have it and are not equipped with it and are not worthy of it, when all the while they are on assignment to get you away from God. Asking for a renewal of these traits and characteristics: yes. Asking like it is new to you: Absolutely NOT!

**HE HAS PROVIDED FOR OTHERS THROUGH YOU SO YOU CANNOT GET TIRED, WEARY, WEAK OR FAINT.**

We are the mentee or mentor to somebody—everyone is. There is someone you are assigned to and there is someone assigned to you. This is a seasonal assignment. This is not permanent in its context. The process is that someone will cross your path who you have a special appointment with and likewise they with you. There are no coincidences and you should recognize that. There are ordained moments where God designs and develops these otherwise "chance" meetings for His good, glory and benefit the future of His Kingdom through you and that person's encounter.

When you meet that person, you cannot be tired, weary, weak or faint. No messenger of God looks this way. That person may think this is not who God sent to me because she is complaining and sour, poor in spirit and weak in love. This is not the characteristic of those who serve the Lord in spirit and in truth. The problem we have is that we are not consistently renewing and replenishing and guarding against empty. Let's stay right there awhile: Guarding against empty. I am hosting a talk show where I discuss various topics and one of them is "Busy-ness Syndrome." This is a phenom I call the interrupting distraction. The "busy" keeps you from your REAL work. This is a powerful tool used you to keep you from your purpose. I posted on Facebook that I was procrastinating. I received several responses telling me to get with it and stop procrastinating. The problem with that is I didn't want to stop. The truth is that I didn't want to do what I was called to do and responsible for doing. It doesn't matter though. I have to do it.

If you do not do what you have been called to do, how can He bless others? What if Jesus asked for this cup to be removed from Him and God said yes? WOW! What would have happened if God changed His mind and the plan? What if I were held completely accountable for my own sins? All that I can say is that I am grateful for the original plan being carried out. I am glad that God blessed me through Christ Jesus.

Likewise, we are to bless others. PERIOD. We are to abandon our selfishness and bless others through our gifts and talents. This is the problem we have as a society. We are selfish and we have our hand closed as tight as a fist and He cannot bless others through us because our hands and our hearts are closed. The other problem is that our hands and our hearts are so closed that we cannot receive the blessings that we are supposed to receive from God through others as well. The blessings which we are equipped to give others should not be withheld. The gifts we have are to be shared. They will end unless we use them according to God's will and with whom He designed.

Tired, weak, weary and faint is not optional when God is at the helm. The average Christian falls victim to tired, weak, weary and faint because we are not seeking God earnestly. The best antidote for the tired, weak, weary and faint is study, prayer, fasting, and meditation. God offers us this provision for the purpose of seeking His will. When we are in His will, we are not tired, weak, weary and faint. We will work hard but never will we be tired, weak, weary or faint. The perseverance that God affords us is spiritual first. The ability to be spiritually strong is a gift from God. The Lord provides rest for your weariness. The Lord provides strength for your tiredness and your weakness. The Lord protects against your faintness.

Jesus has worked hard. He has performed miracles and walked for miles. He has prayed and fed thousands. He is tempted beyond measure. The Man has worked hard. He is never tired or weak or weary or faint. We are not Jesus. I hear your thoughts. However we are made in His image thus we are equipped for such a workload as this. The Lord will rejuvenate you at your request. The Lord cannot win souls when you are acting or being sour, salty and simple. The ability we have to participate for God is a gift from God so He makes provision for the availability of that gift as He needs for the persons you will encounter.

If I were preaching this sermon in a monotone voice, dressed shabbily, with a dry expression, would I be able to help you understand God's words, works or intentions? Not really. You would be thinking I could be watching television or reading or sleeping or anything better than this dry, lifeless Christian. My words would have no power. We are an expressive people. We have to have expressions in what we hear, who me meet and what we share. The same message would not be nearly as effective if I were not as expressive or detailed. You measure the worth of the people you meet by their expressions, personalities and the quality of their conversation. Their Christianity is sometimes an afterthought.

I ask myself daily why does this person need me, why do I need them, what does God have in store for us and what will He use me to do next? These are all questions we should be asking each day for each person who crosses our paths. Why? Because we are always on assignment for Christ. There are no breaks or vacations, no holidays or weekends off. There are no chance meetings or coincidences. Every person we meet is supposed to leave us better than they met us and likewise we are to do the same. In order to do this, we have to abandon the pity party for which we are known and the poor attitude we have married in exchange for the beautiful spirit with which we were born. The ability to share that spirit is the beauty of God at work daily within us.

Divorce the option of tired, weak, weary, and faint for the beauty of God through you. He is able and has done it many times.

### THE ULTIMATE TRUST

**HE INSTILLED LOVE AND POWER WITHIN YOU BECAUSE HE TRUSTED YOU. HE STRENGTHENED YOU BECAUSE HE TRUSTED YOU. HE GAVE YOU SOMETHING TO DO BECAUSE HE**

## An Inordinate Strength for Ordinary Times

**TRUSTS YOU TO DO IT. GO DO THE WORK HE PROVIDED FOR YOU TO DO SO HE CAN CONTINUE TO TRUST YOU.**

God's trust is paramount. He trusts that you will serve the church with your gifts. He trusts that you will serve that woman or that man with the tools He has given you. He trusts you will survive the storm of the economic crisis we appear to be in. He trusts that you will maintain your faith in these uncertain times according to the news and the weather and the psychics. God is a planner. This is not by happen stance. This did not catch God off guard or playing golf or in the mall. God is paying attention to everything that is happening and is already aware of the attitude you have developed in anticipation and in response to these worst of times.

God trusts you! He chose you! He hand-selected and prepared you to do the work which is needed to move His people forward. He could have picked your neighbor. Why are you afraid to do the work He assigned you? He gave you all of the equipment and the tools and the resources for the job He gave you and you are making excuses! You don't trust yourself with the work God has gifted you with. Why is that? Are you not trustworthy? Are you lazy? Are you confused? Are you ignoring God? Are you deaf?

We serve a God who is faithful in the bad times and the good times. We serve a God who understands the situation and He equipped you to deal with that situation and those circumstances with the grace He provides and the love He provides and the power He distributes and the energy He gives you based on faith to exert for His people. As I mentioned before, He trusts you to bless His people. He did not give you that gift to sit at home with that gift or talent.

There are reasons why we do not do the work God has given us. One of those reasons is that we are scared of God using us for His purposes. We are sure of the power which is at work within us. The purpose of our lives is to serve Him through assisting others with their assignments. The glory to God is that we would help others grow closer to Christ. When we are serving God simultaneously, we are reaching Him together. The triangular relationship is a great illustration for this. As we grow close to Christ, we grow closer to one another. In order to grow closer to one another we must release the baggage which prevents us from progressing toward a better obedience to God.

God trusts us better than we trust ourselves. The trust that God has is not based on the emotional traps we set for ourselves and others. The trust we should have is not based on our personal feelings about ourselves—our low self- image—instead it should be based on the image we were birthed in, the image of God. God made us quite capable of what He plans for us to do. This is not a chance performance. He gives us the total of what we need and we have had it for a long time. The trust He wants us to exercise is the one He authored not the one we modified and incorrectly so I might add. The factory settings need to be readjusted. The trust needs to be restored. The original amount of trust we were given to trust God enough with what He wants us to do.

Job addressed the factory settings of trust when God took everything from him. The actions and attitude of Job is our example of what God wants us to do and how He would have us to respond when He asks us to do His work.

He provides us with strength so that we can be trusted. The neglect that we employ is forgetting that He is the source of both.

## CONCLUSION

Only God can provide an inordinate strength. Inordinate is defined by dictionary.com as not within proper or reasonable limits; immoderate; excessive. When I titled this sermon An Inordinate Strength, I need you to understand that God's strength is bigger than we can imagine or understand or generate for ourselves. The God-designed strength is ultimate strength rather than conditional. The God-designed strength is a powerful strength rather than whimsical strength. The God-designed strength is an uplifting strength which revives the weary. The God-designed strength is an experienced strength which revolutionizes the weak. The God-designed strength is a forgiving strength which reminds us to hope in the Source and only the Source.

The God-designed strength is so powerful that it restores us to the factory settings where we can accept His unconditional love, recognize the Source of our strength, and yield to a forgiving God. The God-designed strength is so unique that it elevates us to eagle level: the ultimate symbol of strength, power, and endurance. The strength of an eagle is a unique circumstance because of the nature of eagles. Eagles are removed from general population, set apart. To see an eagle is a rare sighting. Eagles have better than excellent vision. They can see upwards of two miles. To soar, rather than fly, like an eagle is a great gift. Eagles soar high above the Earth using the atmosphere for the ability to fly without much effort. The distance which they can fly without flapping a wing is unbelievable if you misunderstand God. God made the eagle and his ability to soar above with speed and grace.

God can do this in your life if you realize and relinquish to this God-designed love and strength. It is impossible to live a full life without a taste of His Inordinate Strength. The Inordinate Strength provides power through storms and trials of every kind. The Inordinate Strength protects from pain and powerlessness. The Inordinate Strength is a unique provision by the God who loves you unconditionally and desires to give you all that you need to abide in Him.

## An Inordinate Strength for Ordinary Times

God offers us this opportunity daily and lets us accept it at our leisure when we should seek it like water and food and the frivolous things we thirst after which offers no reward. God offers us a strength that He will forever fuel if we submit ourselves to Him. God offers us a strength that offers us continual energy to be dedicated to Him for His works and His will, so that we can be the best servants to Him we can be.

God's Inordinate Strength!

Amen.

# Tools for These Times

*Timely Sermons in Uncertain Times*

## THE STORM'S LESSONS

**Mark 4:35-41** New International Version (NIV)

**Jesus Calms the Storm**

[35] That day when evening came, He said to his disciples, "Let us go over to the other side." [36] Leaving the crowd behind, they took him along, just as He was, in the boat. There were also other boats with him. [37] A furious squall came up, and the waves broke over the boat, so that it was nearly swamped. [38] Jesus was in the stern, sleeping on a cushion. The disciples woke him and said to him, "Teacher, don't you care if we drown?"

[39] He got up, rebuked the wind and said to the waves, "Quiet! Be still!" Then the wind died down and it was completely calm.

[40] He said to his disciples, "Why are you so afraid? Do you still have no faith?"

[41] They were terrified and asked each other, "Who is this? Even the wind and the waves obey Him!"

## THE SERMON

Webster's dictionary defines storm as a disturbance of the atmosphere marked by wind, and usually, rain, snow, hail, sleet or thunder and lightning. Webster also defines storm as an attack. Gage's definition of a storm is whatever moves you off the course chosen by God or self which should drive us closer to God yet has the power and propensity to drive us to other things.

## Tools for These Times

You know how you define storm. It's that "stuff" that you wished would pass you by completely or at least not change your whole life around in one afternoon. Yes, that is a storm. That thought that just crossed your mind. Some of you are in a storm right now. Your children are not behaving or responding to your standards. Your job is challenging your fortitude and if they could only see things your way this would all be resolved. Your family is having one of those silly disputes again. If only they would all grow up and find Jesus, this too would pass. The doctor just delivered horrible and extremely unexpected news. The Lord is expecting you to do things that you cannot discern. All of these events are the definition of a storm—someone's storm.

Now, it is true that your definition of a storm and mine are different. This does not diminish the definition of the either person. The storm is personal and is designed to deliver something personal for each person. No two storms can be compared. What He gives us and what He expects from us is different.

The National Weather Center works diligently during storm season, which is from June to November each year, to study and forecast the storms which are forming in the Atlantic Ocean. Once the storm reaches a certain level of organization, the storm center names the storm. The naming is alphabetical and covers letters "a" through "w" leaving off five letters, "q,"

# The Storm's Lesson

"u," "x," "y," and "z". This naming cycle is good for six years. This naming process replaced the previous one of using confusing latitude and longitude coordinates. They track the storms, project its landfall, consider its severity, establish its category, and compare it to similar storms of our past. There are times when it is suggested that we evacuate. By the time some of us notice that there is a storm on its way, some small Caribbean islands have already experienced complete devastation. They also remind us of the lessons that storms teach us.

Our storm season is not quite that neat. These storms brew and surface at any time. Our personal lives evolve constantly. There is constant need for storm preparation, storm engagement and storm debrief. By the way, the storm does not ask for our permission.

This begs the question and conversation: What lessons do storms provide? Who are you during a storm?

**FEARLESSNESS AT THE PRESENTATION OF THE STORM.**

Here's what we know: the storms do come. We also know that storms don't wait on other storms to end. Storms are designed to build fortitude, establish continuous faith, and remind us to rely solely on God. The first thing in my mind is how, and why is shortly behind. How, Lord, do you expect me to make through this storm? Why, Lord, is this storm happening in my life? Our personal storms do not give warning that it is on the way. The timing of the storm is part of God's plan as well. In order that He may do the work through us He intended, we have to earn this storm education.

As we prepare for the inevitable storms, we should keep some things in mind: a) God has a plan for your survival of this storm; b) God will navigate you through this storm, and, c) you should be prepared to share your testimony about this storm.

Storms are sudden. Unlike the seasonal storms, there is no forecast for our life's storms. V.37 reads "a furious squall came up, and the waves broke over the boat, so that it was nearly swamped." Luke 8:23 reads ". . . and they were in great danger."

By virtue of the scripture, the disciples had cause for concern. But they should not panic. Recall a recent storm in your life. What was your initial response?

Please remember that unapproved moves will take you to the edge of the storm where lessons may never end.

So how shall we behave? Know that the storm is coming. Know that He has a plan for your survival of that storm. Know that the storm will end. Is that all, you may ask. Absolutely not. Storm behavior dictates that we do not panic, but seek the Lord. Remain focused on Him. Remember He is our Center.

The Disciples are not always our best examples of what we should do. After the storm reaches a dangerous level, they panic, yet did ask about Jesus' concern. V.38 reads "Jesus was sleeping on a cushion. The disciples woke Him and said to Him, "Teacher, don't You care if we drown?""

**FAITH THAT THE STORM WILL END.**

The disciples have challenged Jesus with a disrespectful approach. We challenge God all the time when we shouldn't. The disciples basically said that 'You have let this storm occur and You don't care about us as we endure it.' Just like He is present in our lives, He was present on that boat during the storm. He calls us to be faithful, to believe in Him and His comprehensive protection. The disciples woke Him with an indignant attitude. There seems to be some blame, panic and certainly the disbelief in their voices.

Verse 39 reads "He got up, rebuked the wind and said to the waves, "Quiet! Be Still!" Then the wind died down and it was completely calm." Jesus stops the storms in three words.

**JESUS STOPS THE STORMS IN THREE WORDS.**

He responds to our requests, calms our storms and expects us to function with faith during that storm. With that faith, He expects us to believe in what we ask of Him. There are times when He won't stop the storms immediately. He may let the entire storm run its course, all the while we are experiencing

His peace. I personally never want to hear Him say, "O, you of little faith." But He could at any time.

The storm may also grow us up. Our growth is measured by God. He develops us and grows us up through our experiences and lessons, trials and victories.

When we discuss growth, we mean that your life looks different based on your new attitudes, actions and reactions. This translates into stories that no longer shake your faith as they once did and your reaction is no longer the same. Your growth means that your vision of the storm changes. It means that you are going to seek God and respond in a manner that pleases God which starts without doubting God. Growth means that we answer God when He calls immediately and without delay.

Growth means that we are able to share with others how God has moved in our lives. Growth means that we witness to others about the changes God has made in our lives. Growth means that we serve God more intensely, and more intentionally and more sincerely than ever before. God chooses the timing for your growth to be in position to share with others.

He ended the storm. He called us to be faithful. Our response lacks luster.

With a storm survival direction manual, The Bible, and a flashlight, our faith needs to be evident through the end of the storm. Our storm behavior dictates that we remain fearless and

The Storm's Lesson

calm, remain faithful, and finally, fixate our focus on the opportunities which result from a storm.

**FIXATE OUR FOCUS ON THE OPPORTUNITIES THAT STORMS PRESENT.**

I opened this sermon with the definition of a storm with the three of the most powerful definitions I know. I did however leave one off; the most powerful one of all. Jesus' definition of a storm is the ability to get your attention. I mentioned that storms are designed to drive you closer to Him. By virtue of a storm, you will change your behavior. Lesson learned. Don't worry. Don't get worked up and don't panic. I AM GOD. I AM SOVEREIGN. I hear Him.

The storm will teach us lessons. We need to be focused on what those lessons are. "Are we sensitive to His voice?" "Are we obedient?" "Do we respect His will?"

The disciples missed something valuable—they didn't come together to discuss how to better serve Him or how to better share His teachings with others. They were commenting in disbelief of what they witnessed. They are standing there without faith. They are acting common rather than like disciples who have walked with Jesus for any period of time. Jesus was on the boat with them. It does not get any better than that.

It's storm season. Are you preparing, prepared or unprepared?

TOOLS FOR THESE TIMES

**CONCLUSION**

One last note, I am a native Houstonian and have experienced some major hurricanes as a resident. One of the storms was named Hurricane Ike. Ike started off subtly, very quiet. Of the six projections for landfall, they were all wrong. Ike hit the middle of Houston, Texas, at the beginning of the school year. The storm passed over the city within thirty-six hours. That was the longest and most damaging thirty-six hours that Houston had experienced in many years.

First, my behavior in the storm was to move away from the water. At that time, I lived within fifty miles off of the coast. So I took my family about forty miles north. The storm moved methodically at the medium rate of speed. In storm language, this is not good. The slower the storm moves, the more power it can gain, the larger it can get, and the more damage it can cause. The overall desire is to have the weakest in strength, shortest in time length, fastest in speed, and without much power at all. When we consider our life's storms, this is our same prayer.

By the eighteenth hour of the storm, the power is out over much of the city so we are now in the dark. Because of that, we are not able to watch the storm's path. At the twentieth hour, we moved downstairs, not realizing we are now closer to safety. At the twenty-first hour, the situation gets more severe. A tree falls into the roof. The rain is pouring into the residence from the roof of the friend where we are staying. At daylight, we are up

## The Storm's Lesson

trying to stop the water flow into the home. It's like a water works display when you patch up one hole then water spews from somewhere else.

My friends and his neighbors were helping with the roof outside and I was inside cooking to feed the kids. The Holy Spirit said to move them from the table in the breakfast nook to somewhere else so I did. There were seated and eating for about six minutes when the sheetrock fell from the ceiling in the breakfast nook. The sound startled me but the Holy Spirit reminded me that It had me move so that should have been expected. The kids were startled for a few minutes. I had to remain calm, at least outwardly.

I went to survey the damage of the breakfast nook. The floor was covered with sheetrock and water. At once I opened the back door and hurled the sheetrock out. After that, I pushed water out of that same door. My friend and his neighbors looked in amazement and so did the kids. After that area was water free, I resumed minding the kids.

Then we went upstairs to deal with the six foot tree limb over his son's bed. I started picking up the fallen sheetrock at a fast pace. One of his friends found himself standing there starring at me while I was shoveling sheetrock into garbage bags with my bare hands. When I realized that he was staring, I suggested that he resume helping me. I recall asking are you just here to watch. We are to be ACTIVE participants, not bystanders, during a storm.

The storm finally passed and disbanded into a tropical storm then finally just a strong band of rain. The damage lasted for days, weeks, months, and in some cases, years afterwards. The electricity was eventually restored. School finally resumed. Many people returned to their homes, but their lives were never the same. The storm changed their lives forever. Everyone who experienced it has a different story. The changes and the outcome of those changes are different for each person as well.

Most life-altering storms are memorable and become moments we share. That is what storms are for: to tailor our behavior and attitude to God's likeness and to help others persevere.

Amen.

# ON A MISSION OF SERVICE

**John 13:1-17** New International Version (NIV)

**Jesus Washes His Disciples' Feet**

¹It was just before the Passover Feast. Jesus knew that the time had come for him to leave this world and go to the Father. Having loved his own who were in the world, he now showed them the full extent of his love.[a]

² The evening meal was being served, and the devil had already prompted Judas Iscariot, son of Simon, to betray Jesus. ³ Jesus knew that the Father had put all things under his power, and that he had come from God and was returning to God; ⁴ so he got up from the meal, took off his outer clothing, and wrapped a towel around his waist. ⁵ After that, he poured water into a basin and began to wash his disciples' feet, drying them with the towel that was wrapped around him.

⁶ He came to Simon Peter, who said to him, "Lord, are you going to wash my feet?"

⁷ Jesus replied, "You do not realize now what I am doing, but later you will understand."

⁸ "No," said Peter, "you shall never wash my feet."

Jesus answered, "Unless I wash you, you have no part with me."

⁹ "Then, Lord," Simon Peter replied, "not just my feet but my hands and my head as well!"

¹⁰ Jesus answered, "A person who has had a bath needs only to wash his feet; his whole body is clean. And you are clean,

though not every one of you." [11] For he knew who was going to betray him, and that was why he said not everyone was clean.

[12] When he had finished washing their feet, he put on his clothes and returned to his place. "Do you understand what I have done for you?" he asked them. [13] "You call me 'Teacher' and 'Lord,' and rightly so, for that is what I am. [14] Now that I, your Lord and Teacher, have washed your feet, you also should wash one another's feet. [15] I have set you an example that you should do as I have done for you. [16] I tell you the truth, no servant is greater than his master, nor is a messenger greater than the one who sent him. [17] Now that you know these things, you will be blessed if you do them.

## **THE SERMON**

Missions are trips designed to go and serve other communities who do not know Jesus as Lord and assist those persons with the needs they have to expand ministry or simply meet their needs and minister at the same time. With any amount of energy, we have mission opportunities in front of us each day. By definition and design, we are all called to be missionaries. We are charged to serve one another. As we consider the work of missions and missionaries do all over the world. God calls us into particular service to each other whenever we are and specifically through our gifts. He requires us to serve each other.

God offers Jesus as our best missionary example. The God we serve created a Jesus to serve us. Jesus traveled for three years in the ministry when He was revealed as Lord as a missionary—helping, healing, and holding us accountable. Jesus

## On A Mission of Service

demonstrated how to serve others and instructed us to do the same.

In the text, Jesus has been teaching for several chapters. The Passover has commenced in Chapter 12. The Passover Feast is being prepared and is being served. Jesus is shaping the level of service He expects. Verse 4-5 reads: "[4] so he got up from the meal, took off his outer clothing, and wrapped a towel around his waist. [5] After that, he poured water into a basin and began to wash his disciples' feet, drying them with the towel that was wrapped around him."

As He washes the disciple's feet, Peter suggests that the Lord is too good to wash his feet; that Jesus should not be doing such "lowly" things. Jesus as teacher instructs Peter and the disciples that they are clean if they have their feet washed but they have clearly missed the point. Peter, in his usual zealous self, questions the motives and the lessons of Jesus. As Jesus teaches, Peter then understands that he needs again only to wait and Jesus will get to the major lesson rather than the obvious. As we know, Jesus never just represents the obvious. The text teaches about foot washing. How do we regard feet? Do you have pedicures? When your feet are being maintained, are you thinking I could never do this even for money? Yet your pedicurist does this all day to people she does not know. She is paid to do that. You rush to see her because perfectly pedicured feet with sandals is acceptable, while sandals without a pedicure is a fashion faux pas! Bad idea! Likewise, our attitude about feet is not great. Simply put: some people hate feet. They even hate their own feet.

What is incredible is that your feet are a blessed element. The word feet is mentioned several times in the Bible. In one scripture, Psalm 119:105 reads: "Your word is a lamp to my feet and a light for my path." This scripture reminds feet are our transportation. This transportation is important to serving God and serving God through serving others. So we need to adjust our attitude about feet and about service.

Based on our text, we will consider the following points: 1) selective service, 2) submissive service, 3) sacrificial service, and, 4) significant service.

## SELECTIVE SERVICE

We Christians have become selective in who we serve. We only want to serve those who look like us, act like us, are within our circle, and who we find immediate benefit in serving. We are called however to serve those who do not meet any of that criteria. Jesus was found speaking to the woman at the well and she was the subject of all town gossip for her unbecoming behavior. Jesus confirmed the healing of the woman with the issue of blood when He felt power leave him—all because she was not supposed to be in public, and certainly not supposed to be touching a clean Savior with her unclean hands. When did I elevate myself above those who I am designed to serve? Maybe it was when I was asked to lead a part of Christian Education or when I was asked to teach certain classes. Whenever it was that I stop serving others without reservation, that is when I became selective. The reality is that the people who meet my criteria are not the persons who need my service.

When we are selective in our service void of God's assignment and criteria, we have missed our blessing. In our service we are to serve those God sends our way. How do I know? It is this simple. If someone comes to you and you have the gifts and resources to help them, then you are to help them. No matter what! It does not matter. Your doubt about their needs is an indictment against God not the person. God provided the gifts and resources. He determines how you distribute and share. Also because God is the Giver, the resources and gifts are on His timing for replenishment. You are not going to run out while you are in the will of God. The widow lady with the son who was placed to serve Eli and thereafter, that perceived lack did not exist. That applies to us. We need to really understand God's methodology to provide for each of us. He normally provides through others. If you are not serving others, then you are blocking your blessing and possibly delaying the blessings of others. Be clear, God will send that person somewhere else to be served. He will be glorified. The question is what happens to your resources. Will they be minimized because you did not give? We do not know that but what we do know that God gives and God can take away at His discretion.

Jesus selected us to serve. We did not chose Him, rather He chose us (2 Thessalonian 2:13). I have carefully considered how not to be selective. I have considered how I would feel when I get up the courage to ask someone for help and I know that they have the means but say no. That is discouraging and disheartening and causes an impact on my faith. Jesus demonstrated selective service. He served those we rejected. Jesus then demonstrates submissive service.

**SUBMISSIVE SERVICE**

[14] Now that I, your Lord and Teacher, have washed your feet, you also should wash one another's feet.

Our service to others is in submission to Jesus as Jesus has already submitted to God. The reason we cannot be selective but have to be submissive is because He did everything He asked of us. And then some. In our submission, we need to understand what our submission does, where our submissions starts and why our submission is required.

Throughout the text, Jesus is sharing the call to submission. Peter vehemently objects to Jesus washing his feet. Jesus lets Peter know that his full participation is required. Peter concedes as Jesus enlightens Him that this is about Holiness not actual hygiene (verse 10-11 MSG). Jesus plans His lessons well.

## On A Mission of Service

He shows the disciples the full plan. As He trains then in submissive service to others, He realizes that they will be some, like Judas, who are at the table but will still yield to the devil.

The service calls for total surrender to God. This statement begs the question: are we totally surrendered to God and to Christ. The likely answer is no. I know that there are areas that I have not completely given to God. I am not completely surrendered in service. I do not always give my all. 2011 and 2012 have been an exercise and exhibit of how will I submit and surrender to God and do what He has called me to do.

As you consider your life, what areas can you give more of yourself to God? What is He asking you to totally submit to Him? I had to remember, recall, realize that I belong to God. All of me. Everything that I am. My total future belongs to God.

When Jesus shows us how to submit to God, He is extreme. [39] Going a little farther, he fell with his face to the ground and prayed, "My Father, if it is possible, may this cup be taken from me. Yet not as I will, but as you will." Matthew 26:39.

Jesus is asking not to die but totally submits and surrenders to God. We have the nerve to ask Him, is He sure that He wants us to feed the homeless or teach a class, when we are clearly gifted in those areas.

Jesus is submissive and requires us to do the same.

TOOLS FOR THESE TIMES

**SACRIFICIAL SERVICE**

Oh yes! Our service requires sacrifice. We define sacrifice as giving up of ourselves in order to assist someone else. This sacrificial service is what we offer others to give them the best of who we are for the enhancement of another.

When you are sacrificial you put your disdain for that aside. You put your disdain and misunderstanding for service aside to serve others.

When you put others' needs above your own, you have done what God called us to do.

Verse 16 read: "[16] I tell you the truth, no servant is greater than his master, nor is a messenger greater than the one who sent him.

In His serving us through His washing our feet, healing us, and dying for our sins, He shares with us how to serve others. What we give of ourselves is not going to be depleted because we served others. The persons we served also know we understand how to sacrifice for others. When we give of ourselves to others, we show the promises of God.

The widow women and her son had enough flour and oil for one more meal. She was asked to open her home to Elijah and his first request was for a meal. When she considered the meaning of serving Elijah and not being able to provide for herself and her son, she started to say no but she consented. Inside of her sacrifice, God honored her and she did not go without for the duration of his stay or thereafter (1 Kings 17:7-240. God honored her sacrifice! God honors our intent to serve.

Consider Mary's sacrifice! She had so much to lose by accepting her assignment. She was pregnant and unmarried. Her reputation was at risk. But she believed in our God! She accepted her call to service. She became the mother of the child who would later die for her sins. And mine, too! You do not know the measure of your assignment. Be careful when you do not like your assignment. What if Jesus decided to change His mind, heart and soul.

## SIGNIFICANT SERVICE

Verse 17 reads: "[17] Now that you know these things, you will be blessed if you do them."

This verse shares with us that our blessings are coming from God as a direct result of our service. Our actual service is not significant though.

The significance rests on the impact on the life of another. Your service becomes significant because it changes the life of another.

If we return to the widow during the time of Elijah's stay, her son becomes ill, near death. She seeks Elijah. Elijah takes her cares and her concerns to God. The boy is healed and life is returned to his body. There are many additional lessons in 1 Kings 17:7-24, such as faith and the omnipresence of God. For our study today, Elijah is the missionary. Elijah's job was to restore her faith in God. His presence caused her to believe her again. Her faith make her whole again. We do not know what her son went on to do and to become, however we do know that he lived. Usually God takes lives such as his and turns them in something great.

In this story, Elijah is the missionary. He travels with the Word and the work of God. He is not a rich man. God provides for him and directs him. He has a long list of persons to whom he was assigned to serve.

Our service is significant because we change lives. We may cause someone to want to live or want to become closer to God or may help increase their faith. Our service is significant because it changes hearts and minds. Our service uplifts the spirit of another. God does the work. We are just vessels; a representative; the missionary. When we serve others, we have no idea of the complete situation. Our service is at a critical point. Jesus is sharing with the disciples in a short time before a series of events changes the entire world. When we consider when someone has served us, what is the timing of that service? What kind of change does it incite? Where were you mentally, emotionally and spiritually? Were you just about to quit? Were you just about to give up? Were you on the edge of your "cliff" and there appeared to be no way out? Then all of a sudden, hope arrives in the most unlikely person—me or you or some other servant. The significance is that we SHOW up and are obedient to God's will and His voice.

Our significant service saves lives, changes lives, and changes thought patterns. Sometimes we are the glue in lives of others. Let's go back to verse 8b. In these, Jesus tell us that we will have no part of Him. Because He demonstrates this to us, we are able to share that lesson again, and they are able to share that with others. We have no idea what happens when we show up doing what we are assigned to do. The humility and humbleness that we share when we serve are significant to others. We fill the "bucket" of others.

The significance of service where Jesus serves me through others, personally teaches me the promises of God, and loves me on that old, rugged cross.

The service became significant when He washed the feet of the same one who would betray Him. The service became significant when He was judged for being our King. The service became significant when He was marched from hall to hall and found without sin. . . . when He was given a crown of thorns.

When He carried His own cross.

When He was flogged.

When He admitted the criminal to heaven.

When He was pierced and wounded.

When He committed His Spirit to God.

When He died for me.

When they buried him.

The most significant was when He rose and rolled the stone away on a significant Sunday morning.

His service is significant and it was for me!

What a mission!

Amen.

# WHEN YOUR PLAN TO SIN FAILS

**1 Corinthians 10:13** New International Version 1984 (NIV1984)

[13] No temptation has seized you except what is common to man. And God is faithful; he will not let you be tempted beyond what you can bear. But when you are tempted, he will also provide a way out so that you can stand up under it.

## THE SERMON

I love cake. It does not take long to know that cake is my favorite dessert. I make cakes as well so I feed my craving. I make homemade pound cakes and butter cakes and rum cakes. I like icing on most cakes. I own ten bundt pans. Those are cake pans with designs. I have one shaped as a castle and a football stadium. The problem is that cake is fattening. The other problem is that cake is my "go-to," which means when I am down, I want cake. Likewise, when I am celebrating, I want cake too. I really don't need an excuse to have cake. I can have it at any time. For any reasons, under any circumstances.

One morning I was in WANT for some cake. There is this specialty bakery that has cake that I like. So since I was in WANT of cake, I went to purchase a slice. I drove up to the location. I was at the front door when I realized that it was closed! I was too early! I was not happy. Slightly disappointed at best. I was forced to leave without my cake.

## OUR ESCAPE IS A PROMISED PROVISION

No temptation has seized you except what is common to man. God does not want you to sin. Further, the sin in which we indulge has generational consequences. God knows how far today's sin will reach. God does not want you to sin.

Our text shares immediately that the sin you are considering is not new. The issues you have are not new. When you consider your sin options, none of them are new. None of them surprises or eludes God.

Have you ever planned to sin? I have. There are times when I have spent time planning my activity which was sinful. There have been times I have been successful sinning and then I have been unsuccessful in my plan to sin. As you consider your most elaborate plan, how did it come together, only to fail right at execution time? God does not want you to sin.

Our escape is a promise. Keep in mind that since the sin is not new, we also have a record of how they escaped the sin or how severe the consequences are. These lessons should start the persuasive measures required to separate us from sin.

I desire to be in better shape, lose weight and be in better health. So I should have considered the closed store an indication that the cake was not a good idea. This happens in other areas of life, which require our attention.

## The Escape is a Preventative Provision

God does not want you to become comfortable sinning. God does not want us to render ourselves or any other generation cursed because of our sin.

And God is faithful! He will not let you be tempted beyond what you can bear.

God saves us from ourselves and our self-destructive abilities all of the time. When God offers that escape and most often ushers us there, He is saving us for His next assignment and from unforeseen harm and possibly pain.

We can get comfortable with our sin. This level of comfort, with repetitive activity could lead to addiction. Addiction brings harm to the entire family—immediate and extended. You cannot get comfortable with sin. You cannot think that sin is okay because you have been sinning for so long that you forgot it is sin. Sin is the detail He tells us to avoid. Your sin causes curses for future generations—generations you will never meet. You are suffering in some instances because ancestors you have never meet sinned—intentionally or unintentionally.

My errands for the day allowed me to return to the "cake store" after they opened. I had reason to pass back by the store. I was so excited that I would be able to get my cake. That slice of white cake with thick butter cream icing would alleviate my "experience." That cake was the solution—or so I would like it to be. I parked. I entered the store. I placed my order. The sales person stated, "We don't have that one yet. It's on the way through." With a lift in her voice and a zealous smile, she apologized because she looked at my face—disappointed and blank. She had no idea what I had done to arrive there with NO cake! Again, I left the same location without cake. Again, disappointed.

Our text teaches us that God is faithful! We have more than sufficient evidence of God's faithfulness yet He keeps proving it again and again. Now as He saves us from temptation, He reminds us of the God He is to us. God may allow you to be tempted. The text states that He will allow your temptation. His preventative provision means that the temptation will not overtake. Your temptation will be within God's means for you to avoid that sin. The temptation is not designed to show God how much temptation you can bear, rather the temptation is designed to show you and this world how strong you are because of God's provision. This same information shares how much growth you have experienced in your relationship with God.

This is a good time to share that the growth that you experience means that the boundaries established for what you can bear is extended. As we mature and grow, we can bear more—the temptation may expand, extend, or multiply. So the more temptation you experience, the more you are able to bear. With this in mind, you have to remain focused on God and His purpose for providing the escape.

The sin (especially if you avoid it), the temptation, and escape are all part of your testimony. Your testimony will help others understand God better. This testimony is also about the preventative provision—do you share you may be functioning as the escape for the Christian. Your testimony has that type of power because God powers it for that purpose.

God is depending on you to recognize the temptation, Him and the escape. He also wants us to understand why this is important.

God's preventative provision is so we don't have to repent and will be happy to testify about it. God will send hand-selected persons who had that testimony us a means of escape.

## THE ESCAPE IS A PATH TO PARTICIPATING PROVISION

But when you are tempted, He will also provide a way out so that you can stand up under it.

We discussed His promised provision where God knows what you need and He is going to supply that need. He knows where you are and the nature of your temptation.

We discussed His preventative provision. We are reminded of His consistent faithfulness while considering the power of our testimony through His will.

So now as we consider God's participating provision, we first explore the text. God makes a path for your return to Him.

First of all, we will be tempted. Our text confirms that temptation will happen. Temptation is not a matter of if but a matter of when and how often. Further, a matter of what you will be tempted by and what you will do when you are tempted.

God already knew that would be tempted, how you would be tempted, how often you would be tempted, and He has decided what your response needs to be. God knows you so He knows how He wants to build your sustainability.

Temptation is inevitable and perpetual. God provides an escape for each temptation. EACH and EVERYONE of them. Not necessarily in the order they were received.

The question is will you recognize the escape? The next question is will you pursue the escape? The last question is will you share the testimony from the successful escape?

God is going to show you the escape. The point we have to consider is are we objective enough to recognize the escape provided. You first have to recognize you are flirting or entertaining sin. What do you do when you intended to sin and the Holy Spirit gently tugs at you, reminding you that sin is real and can be avoided. When you intend to sin, you need an escape provision. Escapes are positioned as interruptions, poor timing, and schedule changes. Escapes appear like miscommunication and misunderstandings about logistics. Escapes delay your plans or totally divert your arrival. Escapes will appear like something simple however one change can dismantle the entire plan. So now that we have some insight into what an escape looks like.

Will you pursue the escape? Do you want to avoid sin? Sometimes the answer is yes. But sometimes the answer is no. Sometimes we willfully sin. There are times we decide that the sin will be better than the denial. Luke 9:23 states, "Deny yourself." We OFTEN IGNORE these directions. Sometimes we decide to sin, accept the concept of what the consequences are even though we do not know what those consequences are. So as we consider the escape route which is provided, we can think of traffic. Do you willingly go into traffic? Most often not. There are often chances that you do not have a choice about traffic but we have a choice about sin.

How do we pursue the escape? Well the answer to that is not simple but it is easy. No. Learn to use the word NO. Stay out of harm's way. Recognize your own areas of weakness. Keep in mind that your desires—mostly fleshly—are the nature of most of your sin. God desires us to seek the escape, God hopes that we will pursue Him in order to escape sin. God hopes that we will not take NOTICE of the escape plan and willingly move forward with avoiding the sin that tempted us. Now for some of us, the escape is presented differently. As with the cake, the store was closed, then they did have my favorite brand. God knows me well enough to know that there is not a suitable substitute. God knows that the French vanilla cake was the only cake I am willing to use my calories on in that manner. So in order to help—actually to insure my escape, the store was closed. I persisted. Upon my return, the cake was unavailable. Sin avoided. You may be asking why would cake be considered sin. You may be thinking there is nothing wrong with cake. Your thoughts are true except when cake is a "go-to" or activity I indulge in order to cope with my circumstances. The cake represents how I lift myself. This is a sin because I do not seek God for my circumstances. I did not seek God for my needs. I did not acknowledge Him in all things (Proverbs 3:5-6). I did not bring my burdens to Him (Matthew 11:28). I did not trust in Him as my Shepherd (Psalm 23). I did not deny myself (Luke 9:23). I did not seek God totally (Deuteronomy 6:5).

For some of us the cake represents whatever we put in front of God or use to avoid seeking God. In order to pursue the escape, you have to fervently seek God. Be alert. Be aware. Be conscious. Be present.

Finally, desire to be sin free. Seek God fervently so that we avoid sin, which would insure that we do not further separate ourselves from God. We need to pursue God and He will keep us from falling. The ultimate test is will you share your testimony? The escape for someone else may be you. However that cannot happen if you decide that you are going to hold onto the shame that usually results from sin. The solution to shame and guilt is confession to God and share with others as to help them escape the sin that so easily entangles us all. God will guide you as to whom will need our testimony and how we will serve others with that testimony and experience.

Most of the time, we do not share our testimony with others. We are concerned that other people are going to judge us. God allowed that situation—the thorn—so that you will remain close to God, and not get "beside ourselves," a colloquialism which means we consider ourselves an authority on our own situation. We stop consulting God.

God is God. He will receive that which He desires and wills to be done. In short, you will share that testimony or you will share that testimony.

When you share your testimony, you force yourself from bondage every time you share. satan cannot use your testimony against you when you use it to bring God glory. When I say to satan that I am not going to be bullied by you, that means that I will share and there is no shame or guilt which separates us from God. The other part is that we avoid sharing because that means that cannot hold us accountable for future offenses. If we are truly to escape then we need to share so we can repeatedly escape versus escaping and then failing to escape. That is the roller coaster we want to avoid.

In one of my classrooms, I had a student named Chase. One day he came to class and shared that he had been diagnosed with ADHD and was prescribed medication. He shared this basically in front of the class. I asked Chase why he had shared so indiscreetly. He confidently stated that he was not afraid of what anyone would say about him. His transparency inspired me and overwhelmed me into a transparency of my own.

What I learned is when you share your own story, there is no fuel left for others to do so. When I tell you that I have sinned, there is no power when you try to retell my story. You cannot hurt me with my own story.

We have to anticipate in God's provision. In order for the provision of escape to be successful, I have to submit to the escape.

Lastly, "so that you can stand under it" is a wealthy promises from God. "It" refers to the temptation we are to endure or "stand under." Keep in mind that this temptation may not subside immediately. Before the escape, we must endure the temptation. The temptation tends to be great. The objective of temptation is to test you with people, places, and objects. Create the largest possibility that you will respond to the temptation via sin. Sin is the goal of temptation. The result of avoiding temptation is an exhibit of growth and maturity.

When you are tempted, it does not mean that God is going to send the escape immediately. You have to stand until the escape arrives.

God wants you to survive the temptation because your perseverance is being measured, matured and grown. God provides you with standing power because we stand, God is glorified.

Later on in the same day, I found myself near the second dessert location. I became hopeful that I would be successful. However, I reached the location only to find that the location was closed! This was the third attempt for the day to have cake. I do not know the measure of my "need' and my "desire." I do not know the magnitude of the relief the cake would resolve however I do know that God kept me from having that cake. With significant certainty, I can conclude that the cake was off limits. God had prevented me from my own demise and from putting anything before God, seeking comfort and relief in God.

The cake incident was real. I had not thought of it relating until I realized why I could not have it.

God is there when you plan to sin fails, whatever posed as an escape or an elaborate no. God can prompt you to escape the temptation whether voluntary or involuntary.

Your plan never overrides God's will. God can stop your plans to sin at any time.

When your plan to sin fails, seek God fervently. God has something for you to do.

Amen.

# Your Back Should Hurt

**Matthew 11:28-30** New King James Version (NKJV)

[28] Come to Me, all *you* who labor and are heavy laden, and I will give you rest. [29] Take My yoke upon you and learn from Me, for I am gentle and lowly in heart, and you will find rest for your souls. [30] For My yoke *is* easy and My burden is light."

**Matthew 11:28-30** The Message (MSG)

[28-30] "Are you tired? Worn out? Burned out on religion? Come to me. Get away with me and you'll recover your life. I'll show you how to take a real rest. Walk with me and work with me—watch how I do it. Learn the unforced rhythms of grace. I won't lay anything heavy or ill-fitting on you. Keep company with me and you'll learn to live freely and lightly."

## The Sermon

I love these scriptures! My favorite words are heavy laden. There is a song that I like which is sung at the invitation to discipleship and the words are similar to the Scripture, urging us to come to Christ. These are beautiful words to those who are hurting or who have been hurt or who have the potential to be hurt.

Roughly 31,000,000 Americans are afflicted by some type of back pain at any given time, according to the American Chiropractic Association. With so many people suffering from back pain, they are all seeking a solution for their pain. This pain could be real or imagined—whichever, the owner is defining it as pain. We are in pain and are seeking relief. Relief for what ails us. The decision we have to make when selecting pain relief is it temporary and if so, how long can we expect the relief to last, or is it permanent.

Between Advil and Icy Hot, from Ben Gay to BC Powder, there are several pain solutions for sale for the solution of pain. Those purchased solutions are temporary. The directions read do not take more than six tablets per day, take two tablets every 4 to 6 hours, if you are over the age of 12. All of the pain relievers come with instructions and restrictions because these are temporary solutions.

**YOU ELECTED TO CARRY YOUR OWN BURDENS.**

The purpose of your burdens and your troubles is to drive you back to God. You decided to keep the problem with your child, mother, and family. You kept that situation with your boss and your coworkers. You not only kept the problem with your spouse, you hid it too. You kept the health issues and the financial weight all to yourself.

Your burdens, hardships, worries, and fears all belong to God! You elected to keep them but why? Why would you do that? Why would you keep these burdens when clearly they don't belong to you.

When I discussed this with others, I hear all reasons, excuses and non-answers. Let's discuss the top three: you thought you can handle it yourself, it seemed so small, and it was no big deal.

It was no big deal is what you told yourself when you lost your job. You had no idea you would be unemployed for 18 months. You thought with your skills, you could find another position immediately. You consider this a minor issue – not one big enough to bother God with. Now that you have been out of work 18 months, you're wondering what God will do next. He knows your situation and your needs. Why won't He bless you with a job? Did you give Him that burden? Do you trust Him with your needs? Do you consider your life governed by God? Is He not able to take care of your life? Do you consider your problems bigger than your God? Why did you elect to carry your own burdens? Aren't they heavy? Are they heavy enough to make your back hurt? Are they heavy enough to make you give them over to God?

## HAND THEM OVER!

Hand your burdens over! He's waiting. He invites you to be burden free. He's anxious to handle your burdens. Give them up. What do you profit by holding onto some burdens which do not belong to you anyway. The text states, "Come to Me, all you who are weary and burdened, and I will give you rest."

Jesus invites with promise when He says come to me. When I do not give over my burdens to Jesus, what am I telling Jesus? Am I telling Jesus that He is not needed or necessary? Am I telling Jesus that I think that I am more powerful than Him? Am I telling Jesus that He is not able to take care of me and my burdens? Could I be telling God that I do not believe in His plans for me? Is He capable of handling my burdens? Why do I feel my burdens are so special that I am the only person who can handle them? What do I stand to gain by holding onto my burdens?

Jesus says, "Come to Me." Based on that declarative statement undergirded with assurance, I need to figure out how to come to Him. How am I to come? I came to Jesus knowing that He will accept me and my STUFF. I come to Jesus understanding that His love is powerful enough to keep me during these burdens. I come to Him realizing that He is my comforter. I come to Him believing that He is who He says He is. I come humbly. I come willingly. I come peacefully. I come lovingly. I come knowing that my burdens are designed to drive me back to Him.

The verse says that ALL who are. All means me and you. No one is left out. Jesus wants to help us all. But He can only help those who come. This also means that you have to admit that you are burdened and weary. This may be the hardest part of the whole experience. I have to admit my burdens and my weariness. Once I admit my burdens and weariness, then Jesus can help relieve me of those and I can come to Him as He has invited me.

Jesus is not going to beg me to hand over my burdens. Jesus should not have to ask me repeatedly about my burdens.

The question is why do I still have them? What does it take to hand them over? When am I going to hand them over? How was I planning on fixing my own burdens? Who do I think that I am that I can select which burdens, short of all, that I give to God? Keeping them implies that I can handle them or that they are minimal, at best. Hand them over!

**GOD HAS MADE PROVISIONS FOR YOUR BURDENS**

Jesus is anxious to carry your burdens. If He has them, then you could focus on Him and His directions.

When I became a parent, I learned what bothered my daughter. I knew the differences in her cries and what would cause her to cry. I could tell by her voice what was wrong. With this information, I used to "fix" her problems. She would tell me what her burdens were and I would immediately start to solution her needs. She did not hesitate to tell me. She told me everything. As a matter of fact, I often had to ask her to slow down.

God suggests we behave the same way. The text shares with us that Jesus **is** the provision for our burdens. Jesus has an established record of keeping His word.

He is going to relieve you of your burdens. He's going to give you Him to fill that empty place. He's going relieve you of your burdens and offer you His rest. He says that we can wear the best part of Him instead.

The best part of Jesus is His easy yoke and light burdens. Jesus promised the trade. He takes your burdens and gives you His burdens. What burdens would Jesus have? His burdens are defined as living a righteous life, obeying God's word, submitting to God's will and loving God with His whole heart, mind and soul.

Jesus demonstrated that His provision for your burdens is ample when He submitted to God's will. If Jesus died for our sins, then carrying our burdens should be negligible. Your burdens are not bigger than a risen Savior. On top of that, after He dies and is risen from the dead, He still wants our burdens! This is enough for total submission!

So again I ask, who do you think you are that you have decided to hold on to your burdens? What do you think you can do to relieve your own burdens? How do you propose to solve your own burdens? Why do you have a Savior when you do not trust Him with your burdens and when do you plan on giving them up?

## What to Hand Over Immediately

There are some areas that you need to hand over immediately. Hand over:

- your marriage
- your singleness
- your credit
- your kids
- your career
- your budget
- your money
- your house
- your boss
- your parents
- your mind
- your personality
- your church
- your friends
- your dreams
- your fears
- your self-esteem
- your family
- your time

- your bills
- your weight
- your health
- your addictions
- your habits
- your education

Hand over everything! Give it all to Jesus. He wants them. He asked for it!

Jesus invited us to come to Him and He will give us rest. He knows that you are tired. Your back should hurt! But it does not have to. Many of us suffer from stress related illnesses such as heart failure, headaches, and ulcers. Stress also affects your back.

## GIVE JESUS HIS JOB BACK!

When you are taught to lift heavy items, you are taught to bend at the knees. This prescription for safe lifting is taught all over the world. People are shown this video regularly so that the number of work-related injuries are reduced yearly.

When you need back surgery, now you have a choice of less invasive surgery through a laparoscopic procedure. This less invasive procedure shortens the recovery period.

There are many precautionary measures for the back pain we find ourselves in. In our lives, we do not use this type of

## Your Back Should Hurt

caution. We add burden after burden and still want our bodies to perform the same way. We need to give over our burdens so that our bodies can stop hurting.

If I give over my burdens, then maybe my back will stop hurting. My head, my stomach, heart and maybe even my soul will stop hurting! Jesus promised. I am going to give it over to Jesus – all of it. I tried everything else already, even depended on my feeble self!

So I am going to give my burdens to Jesus! He has already proved to me that He can lift me out of the self-inflicted abyss I frequently find myself in.

I don't want my back or soul to hurt anymore.

Amen.

## Tools for These Times

# YOUR FAITH HAS MADE YOU WHOLE

**Luke 7:36-50, 8:40-48; Matthew 15:21-28** New International Version (NIV)

[50] Jesus said to the woman, "Your faith has saved you; go in peace."

[48] Then He said to her, "Daughter, your faith has healed you. Go in peace."

[28] Then Jesus said to her, "Woman, you have great faith! Your request is granted." And her daughter was healed at that moment.

## THE SERMON

You can tell by the context of the scripture that their faith has changed their lives. The women in the context of these scriptures are ill. They are struggling with health issues, specifically an issue of blood, demonic possession, and a sinful spirit. The cultural ramifications of these times are not much different than today. In some regions of the world, there are some of the same cultural stipulations on women. Not being to have her head uncovered in public. Being covered from head to toe so that only her eyes are showing. Not being to able to worship in the same place as the men. The risk to talk to Jesus was huge. She could risk death for talking to Him because of His power and His love for her. This is the story of most women, most of us actually. We are broken. We are struggling. We are in need of healing. We are sinful. We are possessed. The average person has all of these things in the combination that should make us seek Jesus with this same zeal.

The question is are we really willing to love God out loud and in front of others with this same authenticity?

Will you be faithful enough so that God can make you whole?

## SHE RISKED PUBLIC HUMILIATION TO REACH THE SOURCE OF HER HEALING

What are you willing to do to reach Jesus so that you can be healed? Before you answer, let us review some information first. The first thing she realized is Jesus is our source of healing. She made a decision to be healed. There are times when we say we want to be healed but are we willing to take that risk. Are we really willing to be healed? Do we know what we are risking to be healed? She was willing to take that risk! And she figured that the outcome was more rewarding than the risks of the outcome and the consequences. Everything that has a risk also has a consequence. She was risking death and being cast out of her community. She reconciled that she was already at that point of castaway.

Matthew 15:22-28 discusses the daughter and the demonic possession. The text teaches us that the mother was willing to risk her life for her child. The mother is saying that my child's life is worth the risk and is very important to me so that I am compelled to keep her from the demon.

Matthew 15:22-24 reads: "²² A Canaanite woman from that vicinity came to Him, crying out, "Lord, Son of David, have mercy on me! My daughter is suffering terribly from demon-possession." ²³ Jesus did not answer a word. So His disciples came to Him and urged Him, "Send her away, for she keeps crying out after us." ²⁴ He answered, "I was sent only to the lost sheep of Israel."

Jesus says to them that I am here to help her. I am here to hear her cry.

Matthew 15:25-28 reads: "²⁵ The woman came and knelt before him. "Lord, help me!" she said. ²⁶ He replied, "It is not right to take the children's bread and toss it to their dogs. ²⁷ "Yes, Lord," she said, "but even the dogs eat the crumbs that fall from their masters' table." ²⁸ Then Jesus answered, "Woman, you have great faith! Your request is granted." And her daughter was healed from that very hour.

She risked being turned away. She risked being ostracized. She risked those things to save her child from the demonic spirit, something most parents would do. She felt that the risk was worth it. She decided that the risk would win. She could risk it all on the Source. The public humiliation was not a risk for her. She did not care about that public humiliation. She was willing to risk that was available for her child. But we do care. But we do care about public humiliation. We care about image. We consider that what other people think is more important than what God will do in our lives. We care. We harbor that information in our minds. We care. We keep that information in front of us. But she made a decision. She persisted. She persisted in that decision.

Luke 8:40-48 reads: "As Jesus was on His way, the crowds almost crushed Him. [43] And a woman was there who had been subject to bleeding for twelve years,[a] but no one could heal her. [44] She came up behind Him and touched the edge of His cloak, and immediately her bleeding stopped. [45] "Who touched Me?" Jesus asked. When they all denied it, Peter said, "Master, the people are crowding and pressing against You." [46] But Jesus said, "Someone touched Me; I know that power has gone out from Me." [47] Then the woman, seeing that she could not go unnoticed, came trembling and fell at His feet. In the presence of all the people, she told why she had touched Him and how she had been instantly healed. [48] Then He said to her, "Daughter, your faith has healed you. Go in peace."

Verse 46 reads someone touched Me. Jesus acknowledged that a deliberate person is seeking after Him. Peter argues there are so many people around Him and that anyone could have touched Him because there are so many people around Him and they are pressing around Him. The earlier verses read that the crowds were pressing against Him and could have crushed Him. That is how close they are to Him and that is how many people there are around Him. No, no Peter. This touch I am speaking of is a deliberate and an authentic reach for Me. And that reach has a need attached to it because I feel power go from Me. It was transferred. It was a transfer of power. This was not an accidental brush as if we were at the mall or at a concert. This was a deliberate, intentional touch seeking My Power. This touch transferred power from Me to this person and I need to know who it is. And why are you touching Me? Jesus recognized there would be some people deliberately seeking after Him. Those are the stories we need to tell and retell. We need to tell about those who deliberately seek Jesus, the risk associated with seeking Him, and the outcome of your risk.

She was not supposed to be in the general public. We treat people the same way today with certain diseases. She was not supposed amongst people. The issue was thought to be contagious. She however made a profoundly, decisive move and sought after Christ for her healing. She came out in front of all of the people and confessed Lord it was me. She made a decision. She took a stand.

**SHE BRAVED A CROWD TO REACH HIM.**

Two of the three stories gave us a crowd to address these women. We are given that Jesus is on His way somewhere else. And He had to pause to address these women. He was on His way somewhere and the Canaanite woman said wait Lord, help me. The disciples told Jesus that we have somewhere else to be. Jesus responded that He was sent here to help those like her who earnestly and diligently seek Him. He paused. It did not take Him all day. He paused. It may have been fifteen to twenty minutes. He paused because she was brave enough and willing to seek Him. She put image aside in order to seek Him.

In the story of the sinful woman where Jesus was anointed by that woman, there is something special going on about that woman because she is loving on Him.

Verses 36-39 and 44-50, Chapter 7 of Luke, reads: "[36] Now one of the Pharisees invited Jesus to have dinner with Him, so He went to the Pharisee's house and reclined at the table. [37] When a woman who had lived a sinful life in that town learned that Jesus was eating at the Pharisee's house, she brought an alabaster jar of perfume, [38] and as she stood behind Him at His feet weeping, she began to wet His feet with her tears. Then she wiped them with her hair, kissed them and poured perfume on them. [39] When the Pharisee who had invited him saw this, he said to himself, "If this man were a prophet, He would know who is touching Him and what kind of woman she is—that she is a sinner." [44] Then He turned toward the woman and said to Simon,

## Your Faith Has Made You Whole

"Do you see this woman? I came into your house. You did not give me any water for my feet, but she wet my feet with her tears and wiped them with her hair. [45] You did not give me a kiss, but this woman, from the time I entered, has not stopped kissing my feet. [46] You did not put oil on my head, but she has poured perfume on my feet. [47] Therefore, I tell you, her many sins have been forgiven—for she loved much. But he who has been forgiven little loves little." [48] Then Jesus said to her, "Your sins are forgiven." [49] The other guests began to say among themselves, "Who is this who even forgives sins?" [50] Jesus said to the woman, "Your faith has saved you; go in peace."

She was willing to sacrifice. She was willing to be ridiculed for the things that people knew about her from her past. She did not care. She got before Jesus and worshiped Him in front of all of those people. Without concern about what others think about her. She did not care. She goes forward with the fact that this is Jesus and she has recognized who He is. She understands the value of the time she is spending with Him. She knows that He is her God. Without anticipation of anything, He forgives her. She knows what the traditions are. She knows what the customs are. Just as a side bar, one of the other gospels mentions that the perfume she used can be sold and used to feed many hungry people. The perfume is worth a year's salary and she just poured it ALL on the feet of Jesus. All of her time was worth it. All of her sacrifice was worth it. The outcome was definitely worth it. All of her sins were forgiven! She loves heartily. She loves wholly. Jesus recognized the depth of her love. She loved Him with a wholeness that could be copied or duplicated or mimicked. He honored her love and its wholeness.

The lady with the issue of blood broke the law to reach Jesus. She was not supposed to among people. Suppose this "issue" was contagious. What if it spread? What if they caught it? It had lasted twelve years. 4,383 days. And no one could heal her. What if they could catch it, or so they thought. But the rule was because of her illness, she was supposed to stay away from people. She breached security. There were twelve people walking with Jesus. She slipped past, touched His garment, and moved away before the twelve people who should be considered security even noticed. They could not identify her at all. She had worked to be healed. She made decision. She had worked to get to Him and within His space. She was available to be healed. She made whatever sacrifice necessary to be healed.

### SHE UNDERSTOOD THE SOURCE OF HER HEALING

She knew if she could be healed, then Jesus could do it. She knew He could heal her. In Luke 8:43, says that she was there because she knew that all else had failed. No one could heal her. In Luke 8:47b, "In the presence of all people, she told why she had touched him and how she had been instantly healed." She had a why. She had a reason for God. She told Jesus, "I came because I believe that it would be You. Everything else had failed. So if I give it over to You, Jesus, My

## Your Faith Has Made You Whole

Lord, My God, You would heal me. And when I touched You, Lord, I was instantly healed. Instantly." But it required her faith. She understood the weight of that Source. She understood the Lord was the Ultimate Source. If it could not happen with Jesus, it just was not available. It just was not going to happen. If it could not happen with Jesus, it could not be done.

It bears repeating that the risk she took to live was worth her life. Similar to the risk to be saved, she risked her life to live. There is so much weight to that statement. She risked her life. She managed to get through the crowd. Realize that with that kind of blood loss, she should be low on energy and she has had to learn to live on less. She has gotten past security. All of that was required in order to reach Jesus so that she can live a whole and full life. Her faith energized, engineered, and gave power to her quest and pursuit of Jesus. You have to wrap your mind around the concept that there is something more to what I feel is important. Other things weigh more than what I deem important. At that point and time, she was willing to put it all on the line, her chips were all on the table, she was all in. She was willing to give God exactly what He required so that she could be made whole again. If You don't make me whole then my life is not worth living. And everything I risk today is just fine because the outcome is greater than the consequence.

No one knows how long the woman waited for the release of her daughter from this demon. No one knows how long she was demon possessed, but that mother like so many mothers can attest to the fact that we have endured some hardships and struggles with our children. As a result of those storms, we just want them to be made whole and healed. We talk about the storms we have weathered with our children. They are the reason for my walk. That is the basis of my testimony. That season is my reason for coming to church. They are why I am saved. They are why I seek God so earnestly and diligently every single day. As a mother, I do this so that my seed can be made whole. My seed needs to understand the weight of Jesus message and His power. My seed needs to be made whole through my sacrifice.

    The public judged the women in these passages. They judged them for their sins and shortcomings. However this judgment came too late. What others thought, no longer mattered to her. How other people perceived her was no longer her concern. What they said, was no longer of consequence to her. Why? Because she had already survived their judgment to no avail. She knew and understood beyond a shadow of a doubt that those who judged her could not heal her. Those people who judged her could not make her whole. Those people who judged her could not forgive. She knew that those who judged her did not love her. We have to remember that those that judge us do not love us. Remember when Jesus loves us, we have the nerve to question Him and the character of His love. We question Him with various whys and whats and hows. But if we really want to

## Your Faith Has Made You Whole

affirm us, we have to risk all we have. We have to give all over to Him.

### SHE STEPPED FORWARD WHEN JESUS CALLED HER

Jesus is very persistent. We have various examples of His persistence of getting those of us to Him that He has plans for and whom He has called and whom He is here to serve and who He is here to live for. There is a specific group of people who He has said that these are the lost sheep that I am supposed to be able to call unto Me. That is why I am here. He repeats that lesson for us. He is only here to minister to those who are lost and who need me (Matthew 15:24). Nothing else. That is not the reason why. When He called for her after it was she touched His hem and realized that the power from Him was transferred, I wonder how long it was from verse 46 to 47. How long did He actually wait on someone to provide Him with an answer? She decided she would not go unnoticed and she would not deny her God. But she came with honor. She came with humility. She answered Him. She came trembling to Him. She fell at His feet—a posture of worship, in the presence of all the people who she has thus far ignored. Successfully I might add. And she told Him why. She told Him what had happened. How she had been healed instantly. He then replied that her faith has made her whole and for her to go in peace.

Right now we want to discuss the word Daughter. He uses with each of the women. He says to each of them, "Your faith has made you whole. Go in peace, Daughter." The word daughter is capitalized. This is not because it is at the beginning of a sentence. This is an indication of a now proper noun. She belongs to Jesus and He is her God. She has humbly submitted herself to Him so that she can wear the title Daughter. She can only receive this love if she is in the Daughter position. This is a special love is only extended to His daughters. A special love that is not available at that depth for everyone. Just those who humbly and earnestly seek Him. This is an intimate love. Not a regular love. This is only for daughters, whether they are biological daughters, adopted daughters, mentor daughters, and other daughters you have a intimate and special relationship. This is not the kind of love that you give away at the mall or the nail salon. This is a special love and an intimate love. This is the kind of love which you check on her and you pray for her. You challenge her and shelter her. Especially the kind of intimacy where you grant her healing and wholeness and You grant her Your peace. This is not a regular occurrence. Jesus only loves this intimately those who seek Him earnestly! Jesus only heals those persons who decisively want to be healed! Jesus only heals those persons who rush after and say to Him I believe You can do it, Jesus! Beyond a shadow of doubt, I have tried everything else. I have seen other things fail. I have talked to the doctors and no one has an answer for me! But Lord, I know that You are able to heal and You have come at such a time as this for me! To be healed! Forget all of those other people. I am not asking what they think or feel about me being healed. I am telling You that I want to be healed. I know that You are the Source.

Jesus loves intimately those of us who take a risk for Him. He says if you give of your life for Me, I will give you eternal life! These three women have done just that! These three women have determined that His love and His judgment and His healing and His power and His peace from this situation which has occupied my every thought and my every resource and my opportunity and my every moment and my every efforts which has essentially taken my mind from You is now gone. Now I can focus on You, giving You my full attention through the life You have gifted me with. Now I can operate under Your anointing. It is a serious Jesus-styled love that we need to seek, exhibit and embody every day. We need to share this love every day. We need to share with other people that this love exists and that it is real and it true and is worthwhile for what we are doing in our lives. You cannot share love any other way.

Your faith has made you whole. It is time you ask yourself. Do I seek Him earnestly? Do I put everyone on the line when I am seeking Him? Do I consider everything else inconsequential when I am seeking after Him? Do I let everyone know that He is the head of my life and that He is my Father because He calls me Daughter with a deep love? The kind of love that only He can give. The only kind of love He gives. Do I let other people know? Do I share with other people how? Do I give other people that understanding where they can say 'Lord, I want the kind of love Onedia is experiencing from You! The type of conversations Onedia is having with You. I want the type of relationship she has with You because she tells me about You all of the time. ' Does my life reflect that I have a relationship with God—the King? He is King! He is the Wonderful Counselor! He is my Daddy! He calls me Daughter because I have sought Him earnestly! I have breached security to reach Him. I have taken risks which were supposed to end my life but gave me life in order to have Him on my side.

Do we lead a life where we need to go find Him? He has not moved. Go back to that maze that you came out of and go back and find Him where you left Him. Fall at His feet in a posture of worship and ask what must I do to have that posture of relationship. You are already saved. You are simply seeking a reunion with God. You are asking Him what you must do to reach that intimate level of love you desire. Apologize for walking away from Him and His love and His discipline. Help me return to You.

Then He said to her, "Daughter, your faith has healed you. Go in peace."

In Jesus' name.

Amen.

# THE DESTINY THAT GOD HAS FOR YOU WILL NOT CHANGE

**Romans 8:26-39** New International Version (NIV)

[26] In the same way, the Spirit helps us in our weakness. We do not know what we ought to pray for, but the Spirit himself intercedes for us through wordless groans. [27] And he who searches our hearts knows the mind of the Spirit, because the Spirit intercedes for God's people in accordance with the will of God.

[28] And we know that in all things God works for the good of those who love him, who[1] have been called according to his purpose. [29] For those God foreknew he also predestined to be conformed to the image of his Son, that he might be the firstborn among many brothers and sisters. [30] And those he predestined, he also called; those he called, he also justified; those he justified, he also glorified.

**More Than Conquerors**

[31] What, then, shall we say in response to these things? If God is for us, who can be against us? [32] He who did not spare his own Son, but gave him up for us all—how will he not also, along with him, graciously give us all things? [33] Who will bring any charge against those whom God has chosen? It is God who justifies. [34] Who then is the one who condemns? No one. Christ Jesus who died—more than that, who was raised to life—is at the right hand of God and is also interceding for us. [35] Who shall separate us from the love of Christ? Shall trouble or hardship or persecution or famine or nakedness or danger or sword? [36] As it is written:

"For your sake we face death all day long;
we are considered as sheep to be slaughtered."[i]

[37] No, in all these things we are more than conquerors through him who loved us. [38] For I am convinced that neither death nor life, neither angels nor demons,[k] neither the present nor the future, nor any powers, [39] neither height nor depth, nor anything else in all creation, will be able to separate us from the love of God that is in Christ Jesus our Lord.

## THE SERMON

In the New International version of the Bible, there is a header for this section which reads: "More Than Conquerors." As I define conqueror, Webster and dictionary.com agree that victory is the result of the person who is labeled as a conqueror. Victory is defined as success or triumph over an enemy in battle or war. The section header reads 'more than.' More than indicates there is a level above the level we see. More than conquerors implies that we will exceed the victories we perceived or previously experienced. Being a conqueror is enough for the most of us but to exceed our own expectations and capabilities startles even us, not to mention each other.

Get ready for victory!

**YOU WILL NEED THAT LATER**

[28] And we know that in all things God works for the good of those who love him, who[i] have been called according to his purpose.

    Everything that happens to you will be needed later. All of our experiences will be needed later. Either for yourself or for someone else. That experience you have is useful for future experiences. I think that we get caught up in the experience in a manner that our situations are for us. When we harbor that misunderstanding, we lose sight of the bigger outcome. God will use those experiences to minister to others. God uses all of the parts of our lives to grow others. God does not make mistakes. He uses our mistakes for His glory as well.

    When I was in school as a teen, I was a book worm. I craved knowledge, much like now. I remember almost all of the math I have ever taken. I can tutor almost anyone without studying. I never considered that I learned math to reuse it. I learned it because I loved it. Now I share my knowledge with others. For some, this is the least favorite topics: math and school. But we will all need this information again. In the first instance, we will have our own children who may need our help. Secondly, we will need some of that knowledge such as measurement and surface area in our everyday lives. This math experience seems to be needed at the weirdest times. As far as education is concerned, I am convinced that education is in direct proportion to our self-esteem. With that said, when a child asks her mother for help, we do not want to risk our plummeting self-esteem, AGAIN, because we do not know how to arrive at the correct answer. Many educational details are needed. Sometimes they are not accessible to our memories.

The more difficult of the two are spiritual life experiences. Our walk with God. In our spiritual lives, we have experienced some monumental events. These events have been both tragic and triumphant, volatile and victorious. This is the nature of our life and lifestyle. Keep in mind that all events come together to produce a greater outcome. Your trials become your testimony. This testimony becomes what we share with others to provide them with hope. This hope clearly shares with others that God is real and he is in control of the circumstances and the outcome. Our testimony is designed to offer promise of a God who does not lose sight of us in our time of a storm. Storm is defined as uncertainty and trouble, discomfort and upheaval; all while still serving God.

Our measure of need is different so let's consider when someone is talking to you. He starts by sharing that he is having some marital difficulties. He reveals some of the issues they are having. "Coincidentally" his problems are similar to the one you had earlier in your marriage. With prayer and study, you and your spouse managed though that situation, although it really looked bleak. Well the fact that he showed up and felt comfortable enough to share is not chance or coincidence. He showed up because God designed your paths to meet. You are to share the process and steps God led you through so that you would survive. Now it's time to share that so he and his wife can as well. Your trials are not for you. Your trials are so that others can survive with you as an example: you may have wondered with whom you would share this testimony. You may have wondered would it still hurt when you shared it. You may have been concerned would someone else share your testimony. None of that should cause you worry or concern. God sent him with similar marital problems just to you. God trusted that you would share, and not modify or alter the testimony in any manner.

When you wondered why this is happening to us, is was because someone else needed encouragement—only the kind that someone with a similar experience can give.

Remember not to discard or discount any experience.

You will need that later.

## HE MADE YOU IN HIS IMAGE

[29] For those God foreknew he also predestined to be conformed to the image of his Son, that he might be the firstborn among many brothers and sisters.

In the likeness of His Son, Jesus. He made me to resemble Jesus?! He made me to resemble Jesus! This is a spiritual likeness and resemblance rather than a physical similarity. This spiritual resemblance is managed by study, reading, praying, meditating, and fasting. And obeying. A spiritual resemblance requires time and commitment.

Likeness creates expectations and standards. These expectations are not optional. These expectations include reading, God's word, praying to God, meditating on God's word, understanding God's word, and fasting under His leadership. As we consider the spiritual resemblance, that we need to reach, starts with the Bible. What does God have to say? As we hear Him through the words on the page, respond with what He placed on your heart and head. God will share with you what He wants you to understand with the Bible. As you approach reading, you should pray first. Pray for a complete understanding that pleases God. Reading and comprehending is only the initial step, however it may be the hardest.

Hard to read the word of God? Absolutely! This is not a novel and cannot be considered as such. This reading requires undivided attention and an immersed spirit. The work of God has God's voice attached. When God speaks, we need to understand His word, His meaning, His instructions and His expectations. When any of these components are missing, then we are incomplete as disciples.

After you read and understand, we need to meditate on His word. Psalm 1:3 reads: "But His delight is in the law of the Lord, and on His law he meditates day and night." Psalm 19:14 reads: "May the words of my mouth and the meditation of my heart be pleasing in Your sight, O Lord, my Rock and my Redeemer."

As we define meditate and meditation, meditate is a verb which requires action. Meditate is defined to engage in contemplation or reflection, also to ponder. As we meditate over God's word, that time of ponder and reflection should reveal god's direction, God's deliverance, and God's desires. During this time, there is a time of revelation. This is where we wait on answers. This is where we wait on the voice of God. This is also where we clear our minds for God. We need a clear mind to receive God and His direction and His love.

As we resemble Jesus, we need to pray. As a prayer warrior, we need to consider Jesus as our teacher and example of prayer. Jesus first showed us how to pray during His forty day fast. While the Bible does not state that Jesus prayed, we would be shallow to assume that He did not pray during that intense time of temptation. Jesus then taught prayer to the crowds (Matthew 5) while on a mountainside. Matthew 6:9-15 shares with us what we have historically labeled "The Lord's Prayer." This prayer covers important components of prayer as Jesus teaches it. Further, Jesus has a consistent prayer life. He shares with us how to do the same. When Jesus goes to the Garden of Gethsemane (Matthew 26:36-46), Jesus goes to pray three times and each time the disciples fall asleep and do not keep watch.

Our prayer life needs to resemble Jesus! I know this sounds incredible to achieve however, our prayer life needs to be priority. Needs to be cultivated. Prayer needs to happen daily, regularly. Prayer is a talk with God, just a conversation with God. Prayer is a transparent dialogue with God about your life, your needs, your concerns, and your love.

Our prayers need to include seeking forgiveness as well as offering forgiveness to others. Our prayer time is one of intimacy and clarity. Our prayer life is one we should crave the time with God. This time is where we close the gap, eliminate the uncertainty of our existence, and grow up in God's word and presence.

Fasting is the denial of oneself in order to grow closer to God. When we teach fasting, we start with the denial of food and drink and a complete immersion in prayer. Now we include fasting from the phone, social media, the internet, and whatever else that distracts us from God and our ministries. Fasting is done by committing to God your wholeness for His use and cleansing for better use. Fasting is designed to grow us closer to God. Fasting helps us understand God better. Fasting is a learning experience about God and yourself through how God shares information to us. As we seek God for our spiritual resemblances, Jesus shows us how and then provides us the Holy Spirit.

As we are made in His image, we have to eliminate the world's view in our own eyes. We have to be able to ignore the world's opinion and avoid the world's influence. Jesus teaches not to avoid the world's voice. John 15:18-19 reads: "If the world hates you, keep in mind that it hated Me first. If you belonged to the world, it would love you as its own. As it is, you do not belong to the world, but I have chosen you out of the world. That is why the world hates you." We do not belong to the world. It has no power in our eyes. The world has no power over us or within us. We have to reject the world and its advances.

As we alienate the world's view, we will not be popular or well-liked. The world requires us to abandon and distance ourselves from God. The world seeks to destroy our relationship and have us to itself. The world wants to break us and defeat us in order to have hold of us. Jesus died for the whole world but was never of the world.

God made us in His image. In His image. God wants both the world and the Christians to recognize us as His chosen. In His likeness. We should reflect traits and qualities of Jesus because we are created in His image.

TOOLS FOR THESE TIMES

## TO AVOID GOD IS A CHOICE FOR AWHILE

[35] Who shall separate us from the love of Christ? Shall trouble or hardship or persecution or famine or nakedness or danger or sword? [37] No, in all these things we are more than conquerors through him who loved us. [38] For I am convinced that neither death nor life, neither angels nor demons,[k] neither the present nor the future, nor any powers, [39] neither height nor depth, nor anything else in all creation, will be able to separate us from the love of God that is in Christ Jesus our Lord.

Sometimes we avoid God , Jesus Christ and the Holy Spirit. For many reasons, most of which do not make any sense, we try to avoid God, His work, His word, and His voice. For a while He may allow that but that choice can only last for a temporary period of time. Only as long as God allows. WE are shallow enough to think that we are running and this is on our time but in reality, we are on God's timing and under His plan.

Our text shares that NOTHING can separate us from the love of Christ—especially not ourselves and our simple foolishness.

Saul offers us a great example of how God can meet us anywhere and take us anywhere to do what He has called us to do. Acts 9:1-4 is where Saul meets Jesus and is called into change. Saul becomes Paul and is the author of the scriptures we are currently studying.

We avoid God's calling on our lives through avoiding serving others in ministry, and answering His call on our lives. God is only going to allow this as it meets His needs and serves His purpose.

The scripture teaches us to understand that NOTHING can separate us from the love of Christ. Further, NOTHING can separate us from His leadership, guidance, or mercy. As we consider our lives and what God has planned and destines us to do, we cannot avoid it. God is the origin and originator of our destiny and God cannot be avoided. Jesus got Saul's attention with such a bright beam of light that Saul fell to the floor. Jesus knew exactly where Saul was, exactly how to get his attention, and exactly what to do to show Saul who He was. God knows the same about us.

These three verses teaches us that we have to consider those elements which we use as excuses to cause us to distances ourselves from God. There were seventeen elements which the text suggests that we use to establish distance which should be eliminated. Those seventeen circumstances should draw us closer rather than pull us apart from Jesus, instead grow you into a better Christian and closer to God than ever. God can use whatever He wants to draw you close to Him whenever He decides.

Avoiding God is not even a choice.

**A CONQUEROR FOR HIM IS HIS DESIGN FOR YOU**

[37] No, in all these things we are more than conquerors through him who loved us.

The verse starts with NO, which is the answer to question posed in verse 35, which reads: "Shall trouble or hardship or persecution or famine or nakedness or danger or sword?" The verse goes on to address that in all these things, which we just said that cannot separate us from the love of Christ, we are more than conquerors. As we define conqueror, this is a person who will be victorious. In this victory over those circumstances, those victories bring honor and glory to the Lord. WE are conquerors through Him, Jesus Christ, because of Him, Jesus Christ. So we are conquerors over trouble, hardship, persecution, famine, nakedness, danger, sword, death, life, angels, demons, present, future, powers, height, depth, or anything else in all creation. These are the seventeen elements which wish to tear us away from God.

He designed us as conquerors. He made us in His image. Jesus was resurrected after being crucified. We have the appointment of God to overcome the world with its own tools and methods. He equipped us to overcome and He equipped us to be warriors. As we overcome the seventeen elements, we have to consider the purpose God has place on our lives. The purpose could give a hint to what we will actually be faced with. Keep in mind regardless of what it was, we are equipped and we will overcome. Ephesians 6:12 reminds us that we are not fighting against flesh and blood but against the dark world and evil spiritual forces, which would include some of those seventeen elements.

What does a conqueror look like?

Well a conqueror looks like a Christian who studies, prays, fasts, and meditates on God's word both day and night. This conqueror is walking tall in her assignment with her full armor in tact (Ephesians 6:10-18). This Christian is a hard worker, with little complaints and clear direction from the Lord. The conqueror seeks the ways of the Lord (Isaiah 55:8-9). This conqueror can be found praising the Lord at all times. This conqueror knows his gifts and uses them well in accordance with God's word. The conqueror shares the gospel with others (Matthew 28:19-20). The conqueror knows that the Lord has plans for her (Jeremiah 29:11). The conqueror is designed for Him and His wars. God provides the war, the warrior and the victory. It is all God's!

God designed your destiny: for each of us, He designed a destiny. God designed a place for each of us to dwell, thrive, grow, cry, lead, and love. None of which can be avoided. This role is created by God for each of us so that He can be glorified.

Everything that happens to you will be needed later.

He made you in His image.

To avoid your destiny is a choice for a little while.

A conqueror for Him is His destiny for you.

This conqueror looks like you!!!

Go address those choices that God gave you, along with the chances that God gave you, coupled with the gifts that God gave you in order to serve and share Him with and through others.

This conqueror looks like you!

You are who God called to do His work. He did not call someone else to do your work. We are not waiting on someone else to show up to do your job.

This conqueror looks like you!

Your Destiny Cannot Be Avoided

God assigned you! Please get started! God is not going to change His mind about your assignment.

Your Destiny Cannot Be Avoided.

Amen.

TOOLS FOR THESE TIMES

# BETTER THAN I KNOW MYSELF

**Psalm 139:1-4** (New International Version)

¹O Lord, You have searched me and You know me. ²You know when I sit and when I rise; you perceive my thoughts from afar. ³You discern my going out and my lying down; You are familiar with all my ways. ⁴Before a word is on my tongue You know it completely, O Lord.

## THE SERMON

I have known me all of my life, so I know me pretty good. You know yourself well too. Don't you? Sure you do! There are times when people claim to know you better. They have studied your moves, your tone, your voice, your speech and your facial expressions. They ask questions, piece together facts, events and circumstances, and they suggest solutions. These people are relatives, friends, co-workers and sometimes enemies. All have claimed to know you and sometimes even claim expert status.

This is an interesting concept since none of us made ourselves or each other. The practice of knowing another person is a function of what they want you to know and what they want you to see. No one ever knows the whole story. There are decades of research which states that the brain strings events, thoughts, reactions and circumstances together and in doing so, the next time something similar occurs, the brain has a prepared response. When this happens you may be surprised at your research, particularly if it is different than your character. If you are surprised you are going to completely shock others, especially those who "know" you.

There is One who knows you . . . God. Our Creator.

The text is tailored to teach us four important details about us and God. I am not mystery to God. God anticipates my mind, moods, and attitude. God knows my activities and my intentions. Finally, God knows the content of my speech.

Genesis 1:27 states "So God created man in His own image, in the image of God He created him; male and female He created them." As with most creators or inventors, the creator knows the FULL details of the creation. Every nuance, every detail, every special element, the creator or inventor knows. God is our Creator! He knows all about us. Or have we forgotten?

**I AM NOT A MYSTERY TO GOD.**

Psalm 139:1 reads: "O Lord, You have searched me and You know me."

God created me. He built me. He designed me. He constructed me. God made me. God formed me in my mother's womb with the timing for my birth and all of those details are in His hands. I am not a mystery to God. God knows details about me that I do not know. He shares with me about me only what He can afford to have exposed. The only persons I am a mystery to is you and I. We are focused on solving me and others. God already knows EVERYTHING about me. God knows when I'll be hurt, when I won't listen, when I can't hear, when I will need shelter, and when I will grieve. God is not trying to understand me. He is trying to help me understand me. Because of all of this, I will never be alone. Part of our new nature is to avoid being alone, in the physical and the emotional. The reality is that God knew that while He made us in His image, we do not do well alone. God is willing to expose me to myself. God knows us! Stop trying to explain yourself to God.

## GOD ANTICIPATES MY MIND, MOODS, AND ATTITUDE!

Psalm 139:2 reads: "You know when I sit and when I rise; you perceive my thoughts from afar."

God created my mind and as well the crevices of my mind. He knows the contents of those crevices and the intention of those contents. Hand back your mind, mood and attitude to God.

Your mind is a critical element. I think that we need to consider the importance of the mind. The Bible says to be on guard for the devil's schemes. That is an important warning because the mind is the first place the enemy will attack. God is aware of those attacks because satan has to request consent to test, tempt and torture us. God knows what we are capable of and what we can be trusted with. Keep in mind the value of our knowledge, experience and desires are only tested if we are tested. You do not know what you know or how you will respond until you are presented in an adversarial manner in that area of your life. The test results show God how much you can be trusted with and it shows you how much you can be trusted with. The tests also witness to others God's power within your life.

God is aware of what and who triggers the best and worst within you. The caution here is understanding that balance is required. Our Creator knows the good, the bad and the ugly about each of us. When we get in trouble with how to react or respond, ask God. Nobody else can do this for us. Nobody has the intel that God has about us or our future because God created us and is in charge of that future.

## God Knows My Intentions and My Activities

Psalm 139:3 reads: "Your discern my going out and my lying down; You are with all of my ways."

Have you ever been surprised about your own behavior? Have you ever realized that our voice is louder than was reasonable for your situation? Have you ever considered that you are the sum total of your experiences? Even with some prior information, your actions could amaze even you.

Have you ever considered how your surprise others—those who think they know you? With that in mind, Your Creator cannot be surprised by who you are and what you do. Let's be clear that God is sure of what you are capable of. God is comprehensively aware of what you will do now and everyday of your life. God knows your intentions and your activities.

God knows what I wanted to do but didn't. Couldn't. Could not get up the courage to do. When I consider my desires—the thoughts I never share with anyone—God knows that too! With that in mind, God expects us to do several things. One is confess to the mental sin. That thought was the start of sin. God is not pleased with that thought pattern. The second part is that even though we had no intention to carry that thought through, we need to repent for that thought. Thirdly, consider the possibility that God is waiting for you to align yourself with His word. Lastly, we need also consider giving Him our concerns. Whatever caused that thought and those activities, give that issue to God. He is the "lifter of our heads." He has a method to solve our problems which nobody can do like God. When we repent for those thoughts and activities, align ourselves with God and wait on Him to handle it, the outcome is God designed and those results are far better than what we could do for ourselves.

Manage those opportunities carefully. Manage your emotions carefully so that others do not benefit from your emotional decision making. We cannot let the behavior of others cause us to sin. We have to stop making emotional decisions. These emotional decisions allow others the upper hand. Now they will continue to push those buttons and repeatedly push those same buttons, hoping to get the same results. As you allow others to influence you to sin in such a manner—whether a surprise or not—you are giving away the power you are designed to use for other purposes.

God needs to be consulted about all questionable behavior. Let God manage your emotions. Let God move your heart and mind away from the edge of mistake and mishap. Let God encourage and urge the 'best' out of you. The 'best' that He already knows exists. The 'best' that you doubt, grieve and dismiss. Give God your best.

**GOD KNOWS THE WORDS WHICH COME OUT OF MY MOUTH**

Psalm 139:4 reads: "Before a word is on my tongue You know it completely, O Lord."

God knows the words which come out of my mouth, before I know them even. God, for every unkind and unwholesome word that I utter, You already know it. For every word of kindness and compliment, You already know it. For every answer I give in class, for every word I whisper or scream, for every word of comfort or challenge I offer, for every prayer I pray, You, God already know it. God was listening when I said those ugly words. God was listening when I said those compassionate words.

The brain processed output for the rest of the body. Words, sentences and paragraphs are formed with the brain first before they ever reach the tongue and proceed to the lips. God knows the words as they are forming in the brain. As the words are forming, we are making decisions about which ones to use, how those words will affect the recipient. Some of us are more diplomatic than others. Some of us lie instead of telling the truth, thinking that we are being kind. In the long run, we are not being kind by lying.

We need to consider how God feels about the words we use, the people who we are addressing, and how we feel about the words we use as a reflection of who we really are. God addresses the depth not the shallow. We dwell in the shallowness of our experiences. We depend on answers from the shallow portion of our circumstances. God does not dwell there. God is addressing us for the reason why those are the words we chose to use. Are we hurting? Are we broken? Are we disengaged? Are we having an identity crisis? Are we rejecting the truth of who we are, what our needs are, and what our issues are? Are we rejecting God when we use those poorly selected words?

When we make this poor word choice, did God offer us some better options and we ignored the options? Can we use some better words to tell our story, our truths, our observations, our learnings? Can we better express ourselves with the love of God?

Do we know how we can love on someone else through our words? I have authored several books. Within these pages, I have encouraged, testified and shared some very personal experiences. I take care to offer the very best of God's creation. There are people who have thanked me for writing those words and bearing my soul, sharing my spirit, and offering my love through my words. On the other hand, that same mind that processed those great loving words can also produce tears in the eyes of another. Those words are harsh and bitter; dibilitating and paralyzing. The same person can share both kinds of words. The words which hurt come from a hurt person who needs healing from certain situations, people and events. The words which heal come from the person who had been helped and healed in those areas and she is confident enough to share so that others can heal and overcome too.

God is pleased with the words that uplift and restores, loves and affirms, comforts and cares. God holds her close to Him as she grows up through those occasions in which she uses those words. God forgives her when she chooses otherwise. He touches her mind, mouth and soul when she uses "ugly" words. If she is honest, she requests God's forgiveness and He grants it. God reminds her that He loves her, encourages her to use better choices next time and causes her to feel remorse for her misdeeds.

God then sends someone so that she can try it again. This time maybe she gets it right.

God is not guessing or trying. God knows. God knows every detail about you and He remembers everything—every word you have ever uttered and never uttered. God knows every deed, every fight, every grudge, every mishap, every misunderstanding, and every obstacle. God chooses to forget my sins and my arrogance and my selfishness.

There are no secrets I can have from Him, even though I pretend I am successful in that effort.

The text is designed to teach us that we should seek the One who knows us. We should closely align ourselves with the Creator. We should seek the depth of the relationship because of what the Creator knows. The Creator can answer our burning questions. The Creator offers the solution to puzzles of our lives. Our Father, Our Lord eliminates the confusion we have adopted. Our Father, our God provides clarity for existing uncertainty. He has the power to upgrade my self-esteem. My Jehovah provides comfort and confirmation within the confines of our mind and souls to stop rejecting ourselves and allowing others to do the same.

I have known myself for quite some time. So have you. No matter what level of expertise I claim, He is One who knows it ALL. When I want to know how to recover, how to live, what's best for me, and how to respond to the unloving, I'm going to ask Him. The One who knows me and created me. The One who loves me in spite of the modifications I have made to His creation.

Even though I think I know me, He knows me better! He is the EXPERT! He is the GURU! He is the LIVING GOD! He is my Lord and My Father. Now when I have a question, I depend on answers from Him! Only Him!

O Lord, You have searched me and You know me. You know when I sit and when I rise; you perceive my thoughts from afar. You discern my going out and my lying down; You are familiar with all my ways. Before a word is on my tongue You know it completely, O Lord.

Amen.

# GOD'S GPS IS NOT BROKEN

**Psalm 139:5-6** New International Version (NIV)

⁵ You hem me in behind and before,
and You lay Your hand upon me.
⁶ Such knowledge is too wonderful for me,
too lofty for me to attain.

## THE SERMON

GPS is a navigational system device, which helps you navigate streets and areas you do not know. This software can be found in the nearest phone and computer and the internet. This GPS software is designed to help us find our way to different destinations. The GPS software is updated as new streets and subdivisions are developed. The GPS system can sometimes create some laziness within us. The GPS system only helps us to get places we already know exist.

God navigates us to places we did not know exist. God takes us places we would have never been available to. God prepares those places for us and created those places for us. God also knows where we are at all times. God does not need GPS to find us. He does not need GPS and if He needed it, His GPS is not broken. He has not lost track of us. We are neither out of His vision nor His reach even if we seem far away.

God is all-knowing. The God we serve does not need any help finding us or where we need to be next. God has total control of our situation. God's over-arching global presence is what we need to understand as normal, not the exception.

**COMPREHENSIVE COVERAGE OF ME**

[5a] You hem me in behind and before

When you purchase a new car, you have to purchase a full coverage insurance policy. The lender wants coverage for their property. They will allow you to drive their property while you are paying for it, however if you wreck and total their vehicle, they will want the remainder of the amount owed on the car. Notice I did not say the value of the car. Whatever it is worth is less than what is owed, yet they will get paid what is owed. This transaction is a function of insurance. This insurance is full coverage which is a comprehensive policy which covers everything that could possibly happen to the car. If you only had liability insurance, then the car would not be completely covered. They would not be able to recoup their monies which would result in a financial loss. The liability would not be able to cover you from all sides.

This what God has: comprehensive coverage of me. He covers me from uninsured people, underinsured people, and others with His comprehensive full coverage as well.

When I pray, I have this phrase that I pray when I thank God for His hedge of protection around me. This hedge of protection keeps me from all hurt, harm and danger. I pray for it because I know it is there. The process for understanding this hedge of protection is considerably abstract. The process is that we consider the things that we know He keeps from us. That is usually all that we think of. The hedge of protection also keeps us from what we cannot see that wanted to hurt us but God does not allow it. The hedge of protection keeps me from things I want but cannot see the full consequences of my desires. So in essence He saves me from myself. The very desires I have if I got them, I could create my own demise. He protects me from my own demise. This hedge is regulated by God and cannot be breeched except with His permission.

Likewise, God is going to keep me in His sight with the closeness and proximity that only God can have because He is our Creator. God's GPS is not broken as mentioned earlier. And never would be!

This comprehensive coverage includes guarding my heart and my mind from the elements outside which intend to harm me and deter me from accomplishing what God has for me. The comprehensive coverage includes equipping me with His peace which transcends my understanding and yours. This comprehensive coverage includes providing me with support when I have trials of many kind. This comprehensive coverage is a never quit, never expire, never extinguish, never sweat, and never relinquish God-styled coverage. This comprehensive cannot be compared to an Allstate, State Farm or Farmers insurance, nor a Tom-Tom or Google maps navigational system. God will take us places that Google will never be able to take us to.

This comprehensive coverage insures me from the risks I would take but He will pay the price for and have to retrieve me from my foolishness and other issues which will keep me from experiencing His glory and needing His forgiveness.

Just as a footnote, when we took tests in school, those exams were comprehensive. In order to get the best grade, you had to retain and offer the best of the information on the exam. God treats us comprehensively when He loves, protects, provides and forgives us. God knows all about us and chooses to continue to bless us ANYWAY! You know you that would not bless you or love yourself or forgive yourself because you know the wrong you have done and you are aware of your motives.

Finally, comprehensive coverage is going to navigate us to where God wants us to be in a manner which never needs updating. The communion and communication does not need updating like that of the navigational system. The streets are added when new subdivisions are developed. This needs to be updated in the navigational systems through the map programs. God never changes. He is the same today, yesterday and tomorrow. He affirms us, confirms us and steers us with the love and the discipline He promised.

We can never be like God. When I am in front of you, I cannot be behind you. When you are behind me, you cannot be in front of me. This means that you are not comprehensive like God. We have limits. We need to recognize those limits.

God's comprehensive coverage is the best there is!

## GOD POSSESSES ME

[5b] and You lay Your hand upon me.

I had the opportunity to pray for a baby which was thirty-six hours old. I prayed for this special baby which had a very old spirit, a very old soul. The baby looked at me with a certain set of eyes. I never considered exactly what God had planned for this baby. When I opened my eyes at the completion of the prayer, I knew this baby is special and has a special job. I became a part of that purpose. In this prayer, I put my hands on him. During the prayer with my hands on this baby, there was a transfer of spirit. The exchange of the touch included love, information, relationship, and connection. There was a relationship started. There was a rapport built. All fueled by the Holy Spirit.

The New Living Translation reads that 'You place Your hand of blessing on my head.' When God has laid His Hand on me, there are blessings transferred. There is a transfer of knowledge and information. There is a transfer of spirit. There is a transfer of an anointing. And there is further, the protection that comes with His touch. When You put Your hand on me, You reminded me that I already belonged to You. Your possession. Your creation. Your daughter.

So when I consider what God wants me to do, when I consider what He does to protect me, what He puts in me so that He can get what He needs out of me, what He does to extract my gifts at the proper time, when I consider all of those things, I am completely aware that I am not the best daughter He has ever had. I limit Him.

He possesses me. I am His child. For those of you who have children, you know when you tell them to do something, you want it done! Immediately, if not sooner. You want your child to respond to you in a manner which is respectful, respected and knowing and understanding that you are the best authority on what they have going on at this time in their lives. What happens when they reject you? What do you say when they say 'Mom, I really don't think you know what you are talking about. I am going to do this thing my way. I am going to let you know how it works out.' I will let you know right now that you do not respond like God. You do not respond with His grace, His mercy, with His forgiveness or His favor. You do not respond like God. And of course, neither do I.

He possesses us. We belong to Him. We belong to the God who created us. We belong to Him. He has a plan. He has laid His hand upon me. And because He laid His hand upon me,

He affirms me. He reminds me that I am His child. Because I am His child, there are some responsibilities. There are some expectations. Being God's child that means that we are going to have to do some things and be responsible for. Being God's child means we have to take responsibility for things we are assigned. Being God's child carries expectations of others we may not be aware of.

Obviously, I am a preacher. I am a minister. There is this category of kids which belong to us—they are called PK's. The Preacher's Kids. They are labeled that they are the worst of church kids. They do not have the best reputation. But at the end of the day, they are also labeled the most knowledgeable kids. They have to sit in the most church. They have to hear the most sermons. They have to follow their fathers and mothers around when they preach. We expect the most of these children.

Here is what we know. Here is definitely what we know. I am a preacher. I have kids. One day I realized that I have PK's—preacher's kids. Because I have groomed and taught PK's, before I was ever a parent and a preacher, I decided that I would handle my kids differently. I would handle my PK's differently. They are indeed PK's. They need some special support. They are under special attack. They belong to me. There is no doubt in my mind that there is a legacy that goes between generations. There are generations of preachers in some families. Does it come into any surprise that the devil would attack them differently because the devil knows that they are part of a generational legacy?

Jesus said they persecute you because they know that you belong to me. Jesus reminds us that they persecuted Him first.

In the United States legal system, possession represents nine-tenths of the law. When I hear this statement, I have often wondered how did that statement first develop and how did it become popular for people to use it to prove all sorts of unrelated things. The revelation is that God possesses me but not at nine-tenths, but rather at a 100% of the relationship. God possesses me wholly and completely!

God possesses me because He created me and I want Him to possess me. I could have opted out of submitting to His leadership and His possession. Technically, I do when I sin. However, there is nothing that I can do to separate myself from being His possession.

As His possession, He takes care of me. Fully! Completely! Comprehensively!

## Too Much Information

[6] Such knowledge is too wonderful for me,
too lofty for me to attain.

There is a cliché which is TMI: too much information. We use this to say that some has disclosed too much information. When we use this in regard to God, this means that God has shown me His profound measures, ways and actions—more of His profoundness that I am trying to capture in my understanding. In all of Your ways and in all that You do and are, You are profound. When You tell me that You are my hedge of protection, You are completely around me, and when you tell me that I am Your possession and Your hand of blessing is upon me, that is when I have a complete understanding that I do not have an understanding of You at all. That further defines that high and lofty needs help.

In the secular world, TMI means that you have shared too much information with another person and they cannot handle that information. The information has overwhelmed the other person. Now you have rendered them speechless and immobile.

Likewise, we are overwhelmed by God. We are overwhelmed with the things that He does, or we should be. We should be in direct excitement of what He does. We should be in direct awe of what He does. We should be expecting God to overwhelm us at all times. We should expect not to understand God, expect by His consent, what He allows us to. It is not our job to figure God out. We just need to work with what He has given us. We are having a misunderstanding with that. What He makes easy for us to manage, we encumber it by overthinking, and by over analyzing. We do that. So when it says that 'such knowledge is too wonderful for me, too lofty for me to attain,' it means that this knowledge is not common. It is absolutely uncommon. It is never going to be common. It is never going to be something we can explain away with a coincidence or some other phenom which we have attached to science or math.

It is when we get into a space with God where we have totally relinquished the whole concept of we are in control because we are not. We are not in control. Of anything. Not ourselves. Not of anything. When we have a grasp on this lack of control, we then understand that we have to give over that illusion to God. When we remember that God is in control, life is so much smoother for us.

## CONCLUSION

God has comprehensive coverage of me, has possession of me, and offers me too much information. When God speaks to me about where I am and what I will do next, I say, "Yes, Sir." What we have done mistakenly is to forget that He does not need our help with where we are and what we need and what is happening in our lives.

God knows exactly where we are. God knows exactly what we are going. God knows exactly what we are doing. God knows exactly what we are doing. God knows exactly what doors will open for us next.

God is totally aware of what we are coping with and stand in need of.

God does not need our help. God does not need a GPS locator or a software update. God does not need a key map to find us either.

Let God be God.

Amen.

TOOLS FOR THESE TIMES

# HATERS WILL NOT STOP HATING...
# SO QUIT ASKING

**John 15:18-19** New International Version (NIV)

[18] "If the world hates you, keep in mind that it hated Me first, [19] If you belonged to the world, it would love as its own. As it is, you do not belong to the world, but I have chosen you out of the world. That is why the world hates you.

## THE SERMON

Some young people shared with me that a hater was someone who could not be proud of what another person does or discourages another person from doing what they feel led to do. This person who hates on another person does not love themselves. They probably do not have a plan for themselves, which is why they have the necessary time and inclination to do this to someone else.

Haters actually serve several purposes. Their hate is not optional. Exodus 20:16 reads do not bear false witness on your neighbors. This text could be an indication that hating was anticipated.

Haters insure that you stay focused on your purpose. Haters also help you realize how important your purpose is. Haters prevent you from procrastinating and abandoning the effort. Haters require you to maintain your image and continue your journey. Haters would like to cause your plans to fail and for you to QUIT. Just remember that if you quit, they were successful and you weren't. Haters are effective because they assist with your sense of urgency toward the goal.

Haters also remind you of whose child you are, why you are here, and what you were designed for. Haters force you to seek God at all times. Haters should assist you in remembering your Source. Haters are not treating you special. You are not the first to be hated upon. You will not be the last. Jesus had haters first.

## YOU WILL BE HATED BECAUSE JESUS LOVES YOU

Jesus' love causes many things to transpire. There are people who will not love you just because they know you love Jesus and Jesus loves you. Yes, that is all that it takes to be hated. Neither rocket scientist nor medical degree is required to be hated. Just love Jesus. Acknowledge Him as Savior. Serve Him. That is all that is required to have an audience of haters. That is it. You do not have to be a cover model or an athlete. Just show up for Jesus. They are guaranteed to hate you.

When you love Jesus, you automatically reject them. They know better than anyone that you will not love them, if you love Him. They know that best! They are designed to do everything they can to win your love and affection. They try to attract you with all of their available devices. They are persistent. They have no desire to quit trying to get your attention. The problem is that they do not really love you. They just do not want you to love Jesus. They know that they do not have anything to offer that is better or even comparable, but their job is to keep you away from Jesus.

Jesus loves you with and without your consent. He demonstrated His love for you before you were actually born and at the planning of your conception. You were loved even then. So please stop acting like you are not loved, not able to love and not able to receive love. While everyone is not designed to love you, you are called to love others. This love creates action among us. This love becomes contagious and expected. As we consider how Jesus loves us and what that means in our lives, we need to understand how our love affects others.

My love is offensive to some people. I know you may find that hard to believe but some people are offended by my authentic love. This love is offensive because I am transparent with my love. I love others despite of what they do or don't do. This love is without condition. Sometimes I do not realize that I have overwhelmed someone with my love. My transparency causes others to become uncomfortable because they are not able to do the same: love or level of transparency.

Love causes growth—within you and others. Love creates an awesome level of self-reflection and overcomes self-discontent.

Jesus loves you in an unconditional manner. Jesus loves us to create within us a clean heart, the ability to love ourselves and love others.

Self-hate needs to be eliminated as well. This is the worst kind of hate.

Jesus was hated because of His love, even of those who hated Him, persecuted Him, and crucified Him. That is why He is the definition of love. That is why He can ask you to do the same.

**YOU ARE NOT ALONE. YOU ARE NOT FIRST.**

The first thing we need to do is to stop acting like we are the only one who is having trouble or issues or needs. Keep in mind that each of us are tested individually. These individual tests are special just to you. When we ask 'why me, God?', we are saying that we are above the decisions of God. When God tests you, this is a function of trust. God is testing the trust between you and God. God wants to know what He can trust you with. Understand He is really sharing with you what you are trustworthy of. The question is 'why not you?' You are just as worthy of a test as anyone else.

## . . . So Quit Asking

Do you think that people that 'hated' on Jesus would do that again? I don't think so. Could you imagine how they felt when they realized what they had done? I cannot help but consider what they must have felt when they realized that they had beaten their Savior—your own Savior!

You were not first: you are not the first person to be persecuted. You won't be the last. Jesus was persecuted by people who He would die to save. This is an overwhelming thought because we would definitely alienate those we think are our enemies. We definitely would have not pulled them close. That cliché 'keep your friends close and your enemies closer' is not common practice for many of us. We distance those who dislike, misunderstand, misuse, and abuse us, regardless as to why. The call of Christ suggests, or rather, requires that we love all persons, especially those who hate you. The ability to do so is overwhelming at most times. This is not something we just do automatically. Loving those that hate you requires GOD! You need Jesus in this project!

Jesus was persecuted first—before you! He was beaten, falsely accused, ridiculed, denied, and killed. Because you are reading there pages, that means you are alive and whatever you have endured is less than what Jesus endured. Quit the whining—the haters are not going anywhere. They have a job and they are seeking more than 30 pieces of silver as a payoff.

Because Jesus has already endured these activities, Jesus is sympathetic to your situation. Jesus is going to share in your trials empathetically and sends the Holy Spirit as your Comforter. This empathy is given because Jesus cares and is concerned about us. He invites us to cast our cares upon Him for rest and relief. This invitation is for those who believe and who are humble and concerned about His service and commands. Further, this empathy which Jesus extends to us looks like mercy and grace.

Further, this empathy means that He has not left you alone. This means that this empathy extends His support toward you. When He does not leave you alone, that means that He is aware of your persecution and circumstances. While this may be repetitive, it is worth repeating because we need to understand what it means for Jesus to be there with us during our trials and persecution.

When Jesus accompanies us and comforts us, it means that the persecution is something we CAN and WILL survive and endure. Jesus is only to offer us the relief we request but not necessarily what we require. Keep in mind that this persecution may be a test that God authorized and thus He is confident of what you can endure (Job). God permitted this persecution to grow you up in a particular aspect of your life. God has plans for the outcome of this persecution. God often teaches us how to trust ourselves and how to extend our own faith in reference to what we can endure and survive.

Because we are not first, that means that we will not be treated any differently from Jesus. Jesus' persecution and the events He endured make me weep. My events do not compare to what Jesus endured. I know that it is hard to compare and believe that our stuff is not that big. I know that you are remembering your foreclosure, your divorce, your custody battle, your job loss, your broken heart, your abandonment by your family and your homelessness. You may be remembering your rape, the adultery, your physical abuse, your mental abuse, your emotional abuse and your illness.

But if we are honest, we have to admit that we would have failed at being the Risen Savior, the Messiah, the King of Kings, Jesus. We would have asked for the cup to be removed and would have expected it to be dismissed. I would not have suggested "Thy will be done!" I would have been selfish and definitely not sacrificial. I would not have let them beat me, pierce me, hang me or give me that stale liquid. Absolutely NOT! I would have lacked the humility required to be the King of Kings, the Lord of Lords, the Mighty God and the Prince of Peace.

I lack the character which is required to be Jesus.

Further, we don't even speak to people we are related to, so surely we would not allow people who we about to save to beat us. We don't let people brush us in line or passing by. Without haters, Jesus would not have been able to save us. Him saving us required His death.

We fail at being His disciples in some regards—often, so surely we could not be Him. I know I would fail.

Jesus saved those who accused Him, those who beat Him, those who bore false witness toward Him, those who bruised Him, those who hung Him and those who mocked Him! You are not alone! You are not first at being persecuted!

**YOU ARE CHOSEN OUR OF THE WORLD. SET APART. YOU DON'T BELONG TO THE WORLD.**

Ephesians 2:8-10 reads [8]For it is by grace you have been saved, through faith—and this not from ourselves, it is a gift from God—[9]not by works, so that no one can boast. [10]For we are God's workmanship, created in Christ Jesus to do good works, which God prepared in advance for us to do.

If I am prepared for this work in advance, then there is no way we are average, and certainly not below average.

From your smile to your walk, from your ear to your ankle, you are taking blessings from hand to hand, you are truly unique.

## . . . So Quit Asking

When God made us in His own image, He never intended for you to be associated with some things. You are God's workmanship. He built you. Before Ford ever existed, He designed and built your TOUGH. I am supposed to be able to sustain and withstand trials and persecution. He built me to take on my enemy because He is my God! My God, which delivered Moses, Abraham, Sarah, Hannah, Samuel, David, Ruth, Naomi, Ester, and Jesus, orchestrates my steps and keeps me whole, and has a job for me to do. I cannot seem to keep my eyes and all other parts focused on Him.

Understand the part that arrests my attention is the fact that the same world He created, He calls me out of! He does not want me to be like, fall victim to, or be subjected to some things He created. He does not want this for us. We are not supposed to be part of that group. We changed from His original design. Among those who will betray, disobey, and ignore God, God chose you to do some things. These 'things' will attract haters. They are not actually attracted to you but the work you are assigned to do. At a picnic, or any other event where there is food. Gnats and flies will be present anytime we put food on the table. The gnats and flies are attracted to the taste and smell of the food just like you.

Likewise, when you are doing as God assigned, there will be others who will be attracted to your work. Those others, including haters, are designed to create doubt, ignite confusion, and try to make it appear as though your work is unnecessary and you misunderstood your assignment. The more haters you have, the more attention you need to pay with certainty to your assignment. The number of haters and other persons determined to deter you from your assignment could be an indication of how important your assignment is.

As one chosen out of world, your work will not be common. Your work will not be mundane. Your work will be creative, important and relentless. Because you are set apart, your work will be different, often solving the world's greatest mysteries and offering the best solutions for the greatest problems. This special assignment of being set apart is based on trust rather than ability. When God chose Noah to build the ark, collect the animals and wait for rain, God picked him because of trust. When God chose Moses to lead His people across the Red Sea, that selection was based on trust. Even the selection of Sarah to birth Isaac was based on trust even after she had disbelieved. When God selected David as king, His selection was not based on looks, stature, or past experience. Rather God selected David based on a heart which He could trust!

Being set apart is accompanied by huge responsibilities. We have to listen to God—CAREFULLY. We must obey God—PRECISELY. We are charged to share God—FERVENTLY. We are compelled to compassion—without compromise. We are offended by wrong—CONSISTENTLY. We are leaders—

UNAPOLOGETICALLY. We are effective in our areas of ministry—INTIMATELY. Being set apart lacks glamour and fame. It promotes distance and power. The set apart standard gradually happens. This does not happen instantly. It is noticeable over time. David waited several years to serve as king, although was appointed when he was twelve years old. It was not overnight. Likewise, we will not notice the distance until we recognize the assignment, its importance, and the initial impact of the distance and assignment. God distances us because if we had closer proximity then we would not be able to focus on our tasks. Some people have the ability to distract us from our ministry assignments. Paul suggested that we remain single because of this (1 Corinthians 7:1, 32-35). Singleness is definitely set apart. While we are set apart, we can hear God's voice, see God's hand and understand God's messages.

Please do not confuse set apart with elitism or 'better than.' This separation is divinely and deliberately orchestrated by God. By the time you notice the distance, the closeness you once desired will no longer be attractive. No one knows how long set apart lasts, however, Jesus was set apart His entire life. Likewise, so are many of us. So regardless of when we realize that we are, we are set apart. There should not be any thing we would want to do about that.

The world proudly attempts to attack God's chosen but the world has restrictions when engaging in this behavior. When someone belongs to the world, even though the world did not create them, they have a lording influence over them. The world treats its own with malice and contempt but in a seductive manner where this malice and contempt is attractive. The world dangles 'the poisonous apples' in the faces of its own to lure and trap, to taunt and torture. The world defines good differently from God.

God's good, God's abundance, and God's bounty is for His chosen! The manner by which God treats you and the world will treat you will be different. God guards us from being attracted to those elements which would lead us away from Him. The world knows that you belong to God and they know that it has no power over you. The world knew that you belonged to God before you knew it. There are times when we find out that we belong to God because a world representative has told us so. This happens often enough that we are clear that we belong to God, the world is clear and the challenge is different.

Because we belong to God, we are hated by this world. While it does not matter why, the worldly members walked away from God. They walked away from God. They opted out of being chosen by God. When God called them, they ignored God's call. They are too proud to return to God. They are more afraid to be rejected by the world than to be used by the God who created them. This is a tough position and while it is a choice, it is a position we are grateful not to find ourselves in often, if at all.

You do not belong to the world. The world does not have access to you. The world sees you through a store window, and what is in the window is not up for sale or negotiable. The world may want you but God has the final word.

God employs a hedge of protection around you, protecting you from those elements which were sent to attract you and maybe even harm you.

Don't be surprised when you find out how much you do not know because the world was kept from you. People who are teased for being naïve have been protected from the world's schemes. That person's life is marked by favor and power because of the work you are assigned to do. Do not be upset because you do not belong. You have a better place.

## HATERS WILL NOT STOP HATING, SO QUIT ASKING

So quit asking. I suggest often that people leave other people alone. The rule from kindergarten comes to mind: keep your hands to yourself. I often hear Christians say I wish this would stop or can I have a break, and the classic: 'why me?' The answer is why should it stop? The answer is no. The ultimate answer is 'why not you?' You and I, we are good enough for haters to follow us.

With the invention of social media, people who we would label as haters still want to know what you are doing. There is a shirt which reads 'haters follow me daily.' While this may spark laughter, the truth is on the t-shirt. Why do haters do such a fantastic job? They are designed to keep you focused. Without some negative encouragement, you may take an unnecessary break from your work.

So quit asking! Haters are not going anywhere. Joseph's haters lived in his home—his brothers. Sampson lived with his hater: his wife. Job lived with his hater: his wife. These persons have tried to take the spotlight that belongs to God and redirect it to themselves. These haters have tried to take things away which belong to God.

So quit asking! Haters do an excellent job. They do a better job at hating than we do at being a Christian. Haters can be Christian. While it may be obvious to some, it warrants an intentional mention because some people do not expect other Christians with whom you attend church, serve alongside in ministry and hear the same preached word each week, to hate. Since only God can measure the spiritual maturity, we have to understand that they have not totally abandoned the secular mannerisms and attitudes they housed. Further, their growth will include 'putting the hater away.' Although we are Christian, we are still growing which means that we still have to overcome our inability to encourage and support (1 Corinthians 13). We grow to encourage and uplift others even when our circumstances would suggest otherwise. We need each other (Ephesians 4:2-3) We were designed to bear one another's burdens (Galatians 6:2). I am my brother's keeper (Genesis 4:9).

Haters are rewarded by the world for a job well done. There is nothing you can do to change their ability to do a great job. The mistake we make is that we need to stop thinking that if you can 'hate' with so much fervor and such zeal, that likewise your love should be equally as 2explosive. That is a mistake. The measure of great love is not measured by great hate.

Finally, make sure you are not the hater. Reinvent the positive within your life, so that you can be a light to others. Encouragement comes without excuse or prejudices.

Amen.

TOOLS FOR THESE TIMES

# FDIC NOT NECESSARY

**2 Corinthians 5:5** New International Version (NIV)

⁵ Now it is God who has made us for this very purpose and has given us the Spirit as a deposit, guaranteeing what is to come.

## THE SERMON

FDIC, which is the acronym for the Federal Deposit Insurance Corporation, was created in 1933 under the administration of President Franklin D. Roosevelt. Its creation was in response to the failing bank crisis of the 1920's and 1930's. The FDIC by virtue of what it does is supposed to provide security in the mind of the public so that they would resume putting their money in banks. When the public confidence is restored, the economy grows.

FDIC does insure your monetary deposit in any one bank up to $250,000. So you can have more than one account but at a different insured bank and your money would be insured up to $250,000 for each bank in which one person has funds.

There have been three major bank failure periods in the last century: 1920's and 30's, 1980's and 90's, and 2009 and 2010. These major failure periods were responsible for billions of loss dollars. The FDIC has the ability to pay billions out to the private sector for the stability of the economy. This FDIC is designed to insure—guarantee—that your money will be returned in the event of an unfortunate bank failure and closure.

With these three major failure periods, the economic uncertainty rose and caused issues related to the exchange of money.

Because of the need for economic stability or the appearance thereof, many reforms have taken place in order to insure that the money the FDIC has available is enough coverage for any potential issues. Further, reform has taken place to insure that public confidence is maintained. The signs for FDIC participating banks and institutions have to be visible to the consumer. As with anything also, there are limits—limited guarantees.

## ONLY GOD CAN OFFER GUARANTEES

Only God knows exactly what is going to happen next. 2008, 2009, and 2010 were economically devastating to us in the United States. Between war and bank failure, investment fraud and financial scandal, these years caused us to question how America was still a country.

Americans are sufficiently confused that there are guarantees in this world. In the home of the free and the land of the brave, we are severely misguided by our privileged life and lifestyle. So because of the lifestyle we experience and the luxuries we have, we assume we will continue to prosper. We quite frankly expect it. However, we are wrong about the historical value of our experience impacting our future.

God is in control of our future even when we want to opt out. This control is our only guarantee. There is no guarantee which supersedes His excellence. Our assurance lies in the fact that God is in control and His will be done.

God does make some important guarantees! God guaranteed His Son as our Savior. He's the only wise God. That guarantee did not come with some elusive strings and untimely conditions. God saved all of us, even those who led to His demise. With all of that, He guaranteed us a Savior! He delivered Jesus. We cannot get any better guarantee than that! God guaranteed the Holy Spirit! Again, you cannot get better than that.

Part of the American dream is homeownership. Most families want to own a home. They save and save. The families spend time applying for credit and looking for homes. They dream about this experience their whole lives. Mid-2009, the home market did some interesting movements. There was a financing technique called an adjustable rate mortgage. This means that the interest rate will change at a certain point which can dramatically increase the mortgage payment. As a result of that increase, there were many families who lost their homes because they could not any longer afford their note. Secondly, there were several thousand layoffs around the Nation coupled with some international financial crisis. These layoffs also impacted the housing market. These two multi-layered events increased the foreclosure rate astronomically. The problem is that these foreclosures left families homeless and hurting and hallow.

The dream of homeownership ended suddenly for many families. Once they were in the home, they never dreamed of that dream ending. The dream turned reality was not supposed to end. The dream turned reality was not supposed to end tragically. What they never imagined would happen did happen and the guarantee vanished.

God is the only guarantee! There were not companies who could guarantee the homes of those Americans. God is the only guarantee!

## ONLY GOD CAN NEVER FAIL

Only God can make a deposit which will never fail or lose value. FDIC guarantees $250,000 for each depositor per bank. As the economic downturn increased, Wall Street started to fail. As a result of that failing entity, many retirement accounts and other savings accounts experienced severe decrease. The monies to be used for a comfortable retirement for many disappeared overnight. These loses started a nationwide movement entitled Occupy Wall Street. Occupy gathered several thousand protestors in several major cities around the country. Occupy lasted for several weeks until the federal and local police authorities disbanded the protestors. The nature of the protests offered no financial recourse or reparations for the huge financial losses. There are no guarantees.

God makes a significant contribution in our lives as a deposit: The Holy Spirit. The Spirit is active in the Old Testament. However in the New Testament, Jesus introduces and promises the Holy Spirit. The Holy Spirit is a GUARANTEE! The Holy Spirit is provided for our comfort, intercessor and indweller. John 14:16-17 reads: "[16] And I will ask the Father, and he will give you another Counselor to be with you forever— [17] the Spirit of truth. The world cannot accept him, because it neither sees him nor knows him. But you know him, for he lives with you and will be in you." When Jesus promises the Holy Spirit which we know He did because He speaks to us often about the Spirit. Further, the Holy Spirit was guaranteed as an intercessor for prayer. Romans 8:26-27 reads: "[26] In the same way, the Spirit helps us in our weakness. We do not know what we ought to pray for, but the Spirit himself intercedes for us with groans that words cannot express. [27] And he who searches our hearts knows the mind of the Spirit, because the Spirit intercedes for the saints in accordance with God's will."

God and Jesus guarantees what the Holy Spirit will do for us. With so much failing around us, why should we believe what God and Jesus suggest? Because God had kept His word through the Bible. God deserves to be trusted authentically. God has done everything that He says He would. We want to be trusted although we don't do anything we say that we will do. It is guaranteed that one of us will forget, lie, cheat and steal. It is guaranteed that we will be a disappointment to God. It is a guarantee that I will sin.

God guaranteed the Savior, the Holy Spirit, forgiveness, love, wisdom, His peace, and eternal life. God guarantees gifts and allowances and privileges that we could never recreate. His guarantees are powerful and promised. His guarantees are true and real and wonderful.

FDIC is funded on the pay in of the existing banks to be able to cover the potential payouts if the bank fails. This "guarantee" program is limited and can be changed and cancelled at any time. Government programs have the tendency to end, be modified, go broke, and bankrupt. While it is arguable that FDIC is not a government entity, the government can have changes made and other influences to the entity.

God does not operate like that. God is the final word. His policy: The Bible is true and unchangeable. The Bible, a non-negotiable document by a graceful God. God's the Guarantor to all the world. God offers everything that we consider valuable.

**ONLY GOD CAN CHANGE YOUR PURPOSE**

God established you and your purpose and His plans for you as He was creating the Earth. Because He is the author of your purpose so is He the person who can change your purpose. God chose your purpose especially for you, combined with the gifts, He gifted us and has intentionally paired the purpose and gifts for His use and will. Our purpose is to serve Him and others based on what He desires.

Many people find understanding their purpose difficult. There are some obstacles which prevent us from understanding our purpose: us—we stand in our own way. We want to be the author of our own purpose. Because we want that job and it is already taken, we create that friction for ourselves.

Our real jobs are to ask God what our purpose is and seek all the avenues we can to serve in that purpose. What does God want me to do? Seek God for the purpose that will bring God the most glory. Seek to immerse yourself in the will of God! His purpose for you and His will for your life is the same!

There are dreams and goals and desires that each of us have. Some of those dreams, goals and desires will be realized because it is God's will. The success we experience is what God allows. We need to keep that at the front of our mind. We are focused on what we want but that is not being focused on God. God's will has to be paramount. We will only reach His purpose when we submit to Him.

Put your personal agenda aside! I know that it is hard to put our personal agenda aside! I really want to be a university professor. However, if God's will for my life does not include the professorship then I will have to let that "dream" go. If I want to be successful, then I need to follow God's will.

God's sovereignty provides protection that covers me—whether I am wrong or right. So God's sovereignty provides me a hedge of protection. Have you ever asked yourself what is God keeping me from? God keeps harm and danger away from me.

Measure the worth of God's protection. Several years ago I was unhappy with my career choice. I really wanted to leave the retail career. I found an opportunity to leave and I did. I accepted a job with a financial firm, Morgan Stanley. I was training to sit for the Series 7 exam. This exam is a license to sell securities and options and offer sound financial advice. In order to remain employed, I had to pass the test. I had to make this happen. I had made this transition and I needed to keep this job. I studied. I sat for the exam and FAILED! By One Percentage Point! I was devastated! I have never FAILED an exam! I was not anticipating that!

Now I realize that because I failed, I no longer have a job. I had a pending job offer, again retail management position. I accepted the position and worked there for three weeks. That position transitioned me back to my original position. I had to recognize that God meant for me to be there, although I had not wanted to stay. I realized that even though it had been "difficult," it had not been unbearable.

I returned. I was promoted to the next level. I invested my talent for the success of the location. Later in that year, I was napping when I was abruptly awakened from that nap by the phone. My associate manager called and insisted that I turned on the television. I witnessed the second plane which crashed into the World Trade Center tower. While that stimulated compassion because of the tragedy, God immediately flashed that test score in my mind! God brought to my remembrance a series of thoughts which started with "I never told you to leave there but you did. Although I allowed you to leave, I could not let you stay. I know that test score shocked you. I know that you would be devastated, but remember what I did. I brought you back to the place I planned for you." When I sat up, God resolved my mind and my heart. He spoke to me and said: "You had to fail that test so that you could live and do more for Me. If you had passed that test, you would have died in that building."

If I had passed that test, my training would have taken place there in September for the entire month. God's purpose for me is bigger than my desires or my thoughts or dreams.

At that very moment when He arrested my attention with those activities and His words, I had decided to follow expeditiously rather than avoid my purpose with intention.

I examined closely my understanding of His calling and purpose of my life. My examination included putting down those projects that were not part of His purpose for me. God will guarantee the fulfilling of His will and is living according to His purpose for us. God can do whatever He wants to get our attention. In my situation, He allowed me to fail that test so that I would avoid my demise.

We want to consider what God will guarantee and what He wants. I found myself with that company that I had left. But in the end, God had the last word. I stayed with that company for four more years. God defined my purpose. As He does yours. God guarantees the Holy Spirit. God guarantees Our Savior. God guarantees Himself.

God is the only Being which cannot fail. God is the only Being who can change your purpose.

What are we going to do with what we know? What we are going to do with what we know? What are we going to do with this information? The economic climate we are currently surviving as one of a new kind of uncertainty. We owe another country several trillion dollars and our pride. We have more homeless than ever. We have more kids who need care and are without parents. We have more civil unrest than ever. We have a new level of poverty: the middle class. Financial industry changes. More bank failures. Oil prices increasing. We are truly driven by financial prosperity. When that objective does not prove advantageous, then we inadvertently redefine ourselves and incorrectly so.

So what does that have to do with this sermon? While the first answer is the only guarantee is that which is provided by the Creator. The guarantees we have falsely provided for each other are sure to fail. The FDIC is closely monitored so that the Guarantor does not fail while they were invented to provide security. We don't have that worry with God. In our own shortcomings, we have to consider that God's guarantee of the Holy Spirit and purpose are subject to His plan as well.

God reminds us to seek Him for those urgings to understand His purpose and plans for us. We often desire to see the path plainly but that is not how it works. He puts us in places where our own senses are designed to forsake us because our dependencies are misplaced and misguided. Consider what would happen if we really depended on God for His truest guarantees. What would happen if we rested our remaining weight on God and offered Him our complete selves? We are under the misguided perception that we are withholding ourselves from God, when in fact He is actually supporting parts of ourselves that we feel that we control and are in charge of. The very One who Created, kept, and loved, protected, healed and nurtured, is the very One we try to run from. The One we walked away from but He never moves. The One who forgives us but does not condemn us. The One who stands guard at the hedge of protection He formed for each of us.

God expects us to believe and believe in a manner which offers Him the reverence He deserves. God is Our God in all seasons, in all circumstances. God is our GUARANTOR in all situations. FDIC is not necessary and completely ineffective. He has plans for each of the days He has purposed in You.

Amen.

# NEW YEAR, NEW YOU

**Acts 9:1-22** New International Version 1984 (NIV1984)

**Saul's Conversion**

¹Meanwhile, Saul was still breathing out murderous threats against the Lord's disciples. He went to the high priest ² and asked him for letters to the synagogues in Damascus, so that if he found any there who belonged to the Way, whether men or women, he might take them as prisoners to Jerusalem. ³ As he neared Damascus on his journey, suddenly a light from heaven flashed around him. ⁴ He fell to the ground and heard a voice say to him, "Saul, Saul, why do you persecute me?"

⁵ "Who are you, Lord?" Saul asked. "I am Jesus, whom you are persecuting," he replied. ⁶ "Now get up and go into the city, and you will be told what you must do."

⁷ The men traveling with Saul stood there speechless; they heard the sound but did not see anyone. ⁸ Saul got up from the ground, but when he opened his eyes he could see nothing. So they led him by the hand into Damascus. ⁹ For three days he was blind, and did not eat or drink anything.

¹⁰ In Damascus there was a disciple named Ananias. The Lord called to him in a vision, "Ananias!"

"Yes, Lord," he answered.

¹¹ The Lord told him, "Go to the house of Judas on Straight Street and ask for a man from Tarsus named Saul, for he is praying. ¹² In a vision he has seen a man named Ananias come and place his hands on him to restore his sight."

[13] "Lord," Ananias answered, "I have heard many reports about this man and all the harm he has done to your saints in Jerusalem. [14] And he has come here with authority from the chief priests to arrest all who call on your name."

[15] But the Lord said to Ananias, "Go! This man is my chosen instrument to carry my name before the Gentiles and their kings and before the people of Israel. [16] I will show him how much he must suffer for my name."

[17] Then Ananias went to the house and entered it. Placing his hands on Saul, he said, "Brother Saul, the Lord—Jesus, who appeared to you on the road as you were coming here—has sent me so that you may see again and be filled with the Holy Spirit." [18] Immediately, something like scales fell from Saul's eyes, and he could see again. He got up and was baptized, [19] and after taking some food, he regained his strength.

**Saul in Damascus and Jerusalem**

Saul spent several days with the disciples in Damascus. [20] At once he began to preach in the synagogues that Jesus is the Son of God. [21] All those who heard him were astonished and asked, "Isn't he the man who raised havoc in Jerusalem among those who call on this name? And hasn't he come here to take them as prisoners to the chief priests?" [22] Yet Saul grew more and more powerful and baffled the Jews living in Damascus by proving that Jesus is the Christ.

### THE SERMON

Saul at best was a great debater. His persecution of the Lord our God was second to none. The one thing I know about God: He likes the best of the best. If God is going to get someone to do something, He is going to get the best among us.

He is going to pick the best of the best. The one who could be trusted the most. The best representative among us.

He picked someone who was outspoken about Jesus. When Jesus got Saul's attention, He approached him outside, on a road, amongst witnesses, all to get Saul's undivided attention.

Jesus took their best and decided that He wanted their best which they had chosen to persecute Him. When He took their best as His own, He turned Saul into His best with more power, and influence than ever. Saul was now able to influence non-Christians to Jesus as well as undergird and encourage current Christians. Saul has the kind of influence that the ability to create a following and enlarge a ministry.

Saul traveled from town to town to persecute Jesus with murderous threats against those who believed in Jesus and promised that they would be killed. Saul has the authority of the high priest and had followers. Saul had influence and power. Saul was in a pursuit for souls to turn away from Jesus Christ. Likewise, Saul's influence was great and far-reaching and widespread. At the point of Jesus' calling Saul on the road to Damascus, Jesus has already done three things: Jesus trusts Saul to carry out His calling on Saul's life, Jesus has determined that Saul's power and influence needed to be used for leading others to Christ, and Saul does not know who he is persecuting. The penalty for murderous threats and killings should be death. Jesus does something special. He spared Saul's life and CHOSE Saul to bring others to Christ.

Jesus is remarkable at being Jesus and knows exactly where we are and how to get our attention. Jesus does not have GPS, nor does He need it. He knows exactly where we are and what we are doing at all times. As Jesus addresses Saul, Jesus asks Saul the question why do you persecute me. Jesus already knew that Saul was unprepared to answer. After there was no real answer from Saul, Jesus told Saul to resume his journey and await more of My instructions.

On Jesus' instructions, Saul was blind, had to be led to Damascus and went into an immediate fast. Saul had to be led by those who he has been leading. The men were speechless. That action was the start of the transformation which is underway for the men who were with Saul. The fast of blindness, food, and drink lasted three days. This fast was immediate. There was no time for negotiation or escape. An immediate, required fast!

What do you think God revealed during this time? Is this when God reveals Saul's calling and purpose? Is this when God shares His love for Saul and reveals his future? What happens when you fast? Do you fast as God calls you to do? When you avoid that time with God, what are you missing? Fasting is designed to close the distance between us and God. Fasting and prayer are a pair. Fasting is not effective when done alone. That is called a diet or temporary starvation.

Imagine your worse offense against God. Consider what you have done to offend God. All sin is equal. No sin is worse than any other. Our sins are all equal. Saul is not better or worse than us. Has God made efforts to change the destructive direction and nature? How? Have you been paying attention to His efforts? His gentle nudging? Are you ignoring Him? How long do you think you can ignore God?

Jesus had clearly demonstrated that He can get our attention in any manner He desires. Is Jesus' approach subtle or is it Jesus styled dramatic? As we consider Jesus' version of dramatic, I want to be clear that a bright beam of light designed especially for you or killing you child or a ram in bush or an ark or holding back an entire sea is Jesus-styled dramatic. In your life, is it the loss of a child or a job or your deteriorating health or some other tragedy which should bring you to your knees and into a fast? Do you really want God to have to exercise His full Sovereignty because you did not think God was really talking to you or you were afraid of what God is calling you to do?

Is your submissiveness forthcoming or will you continue running or ignoring?

Saul did not have that option. Saul was delivered to Straight Street (verse 11). Where does God deliver you to? Who does God send to you?

As we compare our influences with that of Saul and other Biblical characters, how do we respond? God is calling all of us to a new life. Direct communication from God should arrest your attention.

Saul is not the only one in the text who is transformed in these verses. Saul is trusted because he will seek those who do not believe in God without fear. Saul has the influence over his followers, the high priest as well as Christians. As we consider that one incident in the street, Saul's followers were transformed and trusted to do the same for others. The third transformation was Ananias.

Ananias was chosen to bless the chosen one (verse 10-16). When God called Ananias, He called him definitively. Ananias was ready with a debate. He expressed his feelings to God. God did not offer him any answers or explanation. Again God said GO! In a demanding manner. The way He called his name and the manner God said go, Ananias should not have had any concerns.

Ananias shared the concerns of others as well. Ananias considered what God said after Ananias understood that he was also being asked to trust God that the conversion of Saul would be far reaching, and Ananias was being trusted to participate in that transformation. Ananias had to TRUST God as God was trusting him. Who has God sent to you to help you with your transformation? Have you rejected your Ananias?

As we learn to recognize the transformation we are called to, we have to recognize the persons God use to help us to His will. When people come to you, assume God sent them to move you away from that place where you are not growing or active in ministry.

Ananias did not really want to go see Saul because of what he had heard about Saul. Our 'Ananias' may feel the same way. There are those of us who are hard to approach and communicate with. Ananias was not eager to be that messenger. Ananias wanted confirmation that he would not be killed, imprisoned and otherwise tortured. All of which could be considered to cost of being a disciple.

Who is your Ananias?

Who are you Ananias to?

Who has God placed on your heart and given you directions to minister, to mentor, to help and to invite to have a closer relationship with God? Whoever that is, you are responsible for their next level and you are blocking the blessings of you both. How long are you going to debate and be uncooperative?

Put your name where Saul is. Can God trust you? What is God calling you to do? He has plans for each of us (Jeremiah 29:11). Those plans are ongoing. God moves us and transitions us to the next assignment using various methods. Our job is to be on alert and ready for the transition.

What is your 'blindness' that God inflicts upon you to get your attention?

What does your 'blindness' reveal in your life?

When I consider carefully what God is calling me to do, I remember that I am gifted to preach, teach, pray, write, and encourage. To whom much is given, much is required. With five gifts listed, I am subject to be called on at any time for any reason to anyone and anywhere. God uses subtle gestures to get my attention and call me closer to Him.

New Year, New You.

I cannot not tell you that Saul's conversion was on a new calendar year. What I can tell you is that God can make a new you happen at any time, whether new year or not.

Let's examine Saul's new life. God called Saul as a preacher. Saul's training was 'several' days, which was spent with some disciples in Damascus (Verse 19b) after he spent three days fasting and blind. If I used the contemporary definition of several, several means seven. When I add seven to three, I get ten. If I am still using deductive reasoning liberties, then I am looking at ten days from persecutor of Jesus to preacher for Jesus. There was no debating and dialogue about 'wait God, I am

# New Year, New You

not ready' or 'God, You must have made a mistake. You did not mean for me to preach' or the classic response of ignoring God altogether hoping and maybe even praying that this 'cup' pass away from me.

When Ananias arrived, placed his hands on Saul's eyes, and then shared with Saul that 'I have come so that your sight maybe restored and you may be filled with the Holy Spirit,' Ananias reminds Saul that Jesus appeared to Him, as if Saul had any doubt. One important note: Jesus really did not need Ananias to restore Saul's sight. Ananias needed to witness God's miraculous transformation as well. God needs someone He could trust to tell what happened. Ananias had the personality which stated that 'I am about facts and cannot take certain chances.'

The new Saul was preaching in about ten days. In this relatively short period of preparation, the word spreads that a significant conversion has taken place. When he is done with the Damascus disciples, Saul "immediately" starts to preach the gospel of Jesus (verse 20). As a preacher called by God, saved by Jesus and filled with the Holy Spirit, I did not answer immediately and I did not immediately preach. I procrastinated and avoided and tried to ignore God. This lasted about 1500 days. How long did you run, avoid, and ignore God?

The new Saul was already transitioned from persecuted to preacher with new witnesses who could clearly articulate his past. Verse 21 states: "All those who heard him were astonished and asked, "Isn't he the man who raised havoc in Jerusalem among those who call on this name? And hasn't he come here to take them as prisoners to the chief priests?" God showed these witnesses what God can through a previous unbeliever. Saul serves God as an example that God can use anyone He chooses at anytime. God shares with us this event that NO ONE is lost across enemy lines.

God's plans for the new you cannot be stopped by anyone; not even you. We thank God for Saul who turned Paul because this previous persecutor authored half of the New Testament. We thank God for Saul turned Paul because he prays for us and teaches us to pray.

As we consider that new you, what will we thank God for regarding your life? What will we praise God for because You followed God to your new you?

    What does the new you do?

    What does the new you look like?

    What does the new you sound like?

    What does the new you say?

    Where does the new you go?

    Who does the new you serve?

    Does the new you love better?

Does the new you love God more?

Does the new you pray more? Deeper? More authentic?

Does the new you access more spiritual gifts?

Does the new you obey quicker?

Does the new you recognize the voice of God?

Do others question your newness?

Do others challenge our new ministry role?

Who are you Ananias to?

Does the new you ever try to return to the old you?

New Year New You!

What is God moving you to do?

Remember the last transition you experienced? God made it work—it was not easy but it was wonderful. God smoothed the rough spots—He made the crooked places straight.

God used the best part of you to give Him the best part of you. And you were present. And willing. And cooperative. And effective.

Verse 22 reads: "Yet Saul grew more and more powerful and baffled the Jews living in Damascus by proving that Jesus is the Christ." That power Saul has come from Jesus. As He will be with us as we submit to our new year, new you. God fuels what He has called forth and ordained.

God will get the glory, the honor, and all the praise. Our God is an awesome God. He reigns from Heaven above. Our God is awesome. He can move mountains. Keeps me in the valley. Hides me from the rain. Heals me when I'm broken. Forever He will reign. My God is awesome. God created me to serve, glorify, and magnify Him.

He selects those He trusts. Those He knows will do what He desires. His choices and ours are so significantly different. We may not always understand why He chose some people—sometimes we do not understand why He chose us—and it is not for us to understand. God uses those of us who believes what God says. God uses those of us with a zeal and fervency toward God.

God can create within us a clean heart. A heart to be used for His glory.

New Year, New You!

Amen.

# Resources

They Like to Never Quit Praising God by Frank Thomas

The Homiletical Plot by Eugene L. Lowry

Celebration and Experience in Preaching by Henry H. Mitchell

The Certain Sound of the Trumpet by Samuel Proctor

360 Degree Preaching by Michael J. Quicke

Expository Preaching by Haddon Robinson

The In Between Times by Ralph D. West, Sr.

The Four Pages of the Sermon by Paul Scott Wilson

# TOOLS FOR THESE TIMES

# Acknowledgements

God, thank You for Your plans for me. Thank You for ***Tools for These Times*** and choosing me to complete Your project. I just want to please You. Thank You for continuing to anoint me and to invest in me and my gifts, which keep surprising me. Thank You for loving and forgiving me.

Hillary and Nehemiah, thank you for supporting me and my endeavors. Thank you for loving me, especially when I do nothing without a pen and a clipboard, thank you for enduring my late nights, your ideas, the sounding board, the love and the support. Thank you for celebrating our legacy.

Kimberly 'Ann' Joiner, thank you for reading my work and offering your honest feedback. May your life be blessed by me doing God's will.

To my prayer partners and to my accountability partners, thank you for the long talks and the powerful prayers and the encouragement. To my pastor and church family, thank you so much for your love and support.

# TOOLS FOR THESE TIMES

Minister Onedia N. Gage seeks to share her study and motivation with you in her outlandish pursuit of God. She desires to share her faith in a manner which helps you do the same. She hopes that these words bless you.

Please feel free to contact and share your testimony.
onediagage@onediagage.com or @onediangage (twitter).
www.onediagage.com

Blogtalkradio.com/onediagage

Youtube.com/onediagage

Facebook.com/onediagageministries

Facebook.com/onedia-n-gage

# Tools for These Times

*Timely Sermons in Uncertain Times*

# Publishing

Do you have a book you want to write, but do not know what to do?

Do you have a book you need to publish but do not know how to start?

Would publishing move your career forward?

Let us help

onediagage@purpleink.net ♦ www.purpleink.net

## 512.715.4243